nihongo notes 4

understanding communication in japanese

by
osamu mizutani
nobuko mizutani

The Japan Times

First edition: December 1981
Seventh printing: May 1988

Jacket design by Koji Detake

ISBN4-7890-0160-1

Published by The Japan Times, Ltd.
5-4, Shibaura 4-chome, Minato-ku, Tokyo 108, Japan

Printed in Japan

FOREWORD

This book is a compilation of the seventy columns which appeared in *The Japan Times* from August 10, 1980 to December 6, 1981 under the title "Nihongo Notes." (The preceding 210 columns have been published as *Nihongo Notes 1, 2* and *3*.) We have also added a list of basic example sentences and explanations entitled "Guide for Avoidance of Common Mistakes" as a supplement to these columns.

In this volume, while continuing to explain the actual usage of various Japanese expressions, we have attempted to take up more specific situations and to provide more detailed explanations. The columns in this volume deal with such diverse aspects of Japanese usage as expressions used at ceremonial occasions like wedding parties, expressions used to reinforce the feeling of belonging to the same group, expressions used for implicitly conveying one's requests, emphatic expressions of one's feelings, and important nonverbal expressions like bowing and knocking.

It is a great pleasure to be able to publish another volume of *Nihongo Notes*. We hope that you will enjoy reading it and find some help in understanding more about how Japanese use their language.

We would like to acknowledge the help of Janet Ashby who checked the English for these columns and offered valuable suggestions just as she did for the preceding three volumes.

December, 1981
Osamu and Nobuko Mizutani

CONTENTS

Note Concerning Romanization

The romanization used in this book (as well as in *An Introduction to Modern Japanese*) is based on the Hepburn system with the following modifications.

1. When the same vowel occurs con-secutively, the letter is repeated rather than using the "-" mark.
   ex. *Tookyoo*   (instead of *Tōkyō*)
2. The sound indicated by the hiragana ん is written with "*n*" regardless of what sound follows it.
   ex. *shinbun*   (instead of shimbun)
   ex. *shinpai*   (instead of shimpai)

The words connected with hyphens are pro-nounced as one unit.
   ex. *genki-desu*
   ex. *Soo-desu-ne*

Sasoimashoo
さそいましょう
(Let's ask her to go with us)

The other day Mr. Lerner, Mr. Takada, and Miss Yoshida were planning a picnic. Miss Yoshida said that she would like to have another woman go with them, so Mr. Lerner suggested asking along one of her friends, Miss Matsumoto, saying

Matsumoto-san-mo tanomimashoo-ka.

meaning "Shall we ask Miss Matsumoto, too?" Mr. Takada repeated *Tanomu?* (Ask?), but Miss Yoshida quickly understood as usual, and said

Soo-desu-ne. Matsumoto-san-mo sasoimashoo-yo.
そうですね。松本さんも　さそいましょうよ。
(That's right. Let's ask Miss Matsumoto, too.)

Mr. Lerner remembered that he had learned the word *sasou*, but had not used it himself; he finds it difficult to choose the correct word from the several that seem to be equivalent to the English "ask."

*　　*　　*

Just as the Japanese word *kiku* has various meanings in English, the English "ask" has more than one Japanese word to correspond to it. To ask questions, one uses *kiku* as in *Matsumoto-san-ni kikimasu* (I'll ask Miss Matsumoto about it) or *shitsumon-shimasu* or *tazunemasu.* (Among these three verbs, *kiku* is used most often.) *Ta-*

nomu is used to mean "to request someone to do something" as in

A: *Isogashikute zenbu-wa dekinai-kamo shirema-sen.*

(I'm so busy that I may not be able to do all of it.)

B: *Ja, Matsumoto-san-ni hanbun tanomimashoo.*

(Then I'll ask Miss Matsumoto to do half.)

More politely, *onegai-suru* is used in place of *tanomu.*

On the other hand, when you invite someone out, you should use the word *sasou.* (To invite someone to your house, *yobu* or *maneku* is used.) And when you are invited out and can't go, you can say, after declining the invitation

Mata kondo sasotte-kudasai.
また　こんど　さそってください。
(Please ask me again some time.)

Although *Matsumoto-san-mo sasoimashoo* is a brief expression to mean "Let's ask Miss Matsumoto too," you can say this using *kiku* also, as in

Issho-ni itte-kureru-ka dooka Matsumoto-san-ni kiite-mimashoo.

(Let's ask Miss Matsumoto if she can go with us.)

Otomo-shimasu
お供します
(I'll go with you)

Miss Winters, Mr. Lerner's friend, wanted to invite Mr. Mori, the director of Mr. Lerner's company, to a party at her house, and asked him to convey her invitation to him. Mr. Lerner went to Mr. Mori, and asked him to go to the party. Mr. Mori said that he would like to go, and asked

Raanaa-san-mo issho-ni itte-kureru-n-deshoo-ne.
(I presume you will go with me.)

When Mr. Lerner said yes, Mr. Mori told him

Ja, tsurete-itte-kudasai.
(Well, then, please take me.)

Relieved, Mr. Lerner started saying *Hai, tsurete-itte-agemasu* to mean "Yes, I will be glad to take you there," and wondered if *sashiageru* should be used instead of *ageru*. When he asked Miss Yoshida about it, she said he should have said

Otomo-shimasu. お供します。

instead.

* * *

When one does not have to be polite, it is very simple to invite someone out. One simply says *Issho-ni ikimasen-ka* (Won't you go with me?) and the other person says *Ee, ikimashoo* (Yes, I will). The verb *iku* can be used by both the speaker and the listener. But when you have

10

to be polite, you should use some other expression to refer to the other person's going such as *irassharu* or *oide-ni naru*.

It is all right to say *Issho-ni irasshaimasen-ka* to mean "Won't you go with me?" when you don't have to be very polite. But strictly speaking, the verb *irassharu* or *oide-ni naru* cannot be used for the speaker, and some other verb must be used. So when you have to be very polite or formal, you should use two sentences with two different verbs as in:

Irasshaimasen-ka (or Oide-ni narimasen-ka).
Watashi-mo mairimasu.
(Would you like to go? I will go, too.)

Or, *Otomo-shimasu* (I will follow you) can be used in place of *Watashi-mo mairimasu.* (Some people think that *otomo-suru* sounds too formal and prefer *goissho-suru*.)

Chotto oshiete-kudasai
ちょっと　教えてください
(Please show me how to do it)

A few days ago Mr. Lerner noticed that there was a new copying machine near Miss Yoshida's desk. He tried to copy some papers on it himself, but he did not know exactly how to work it, so he asked her

Tsukaikata-ga wakarimasen-kara, chotto misete-kudasai.

meaning "Since I don't know how to use it, please show me how to do it." Miss Yoshida took out a booklet from her desk, but before she had handed it to him, she realized what he meant, and said

Tsukaikata-o oshiete-agemashoo-ka.
使い方を　教えてあげましようか。
(Shall I show you how to use it?)

Mr. Lerner thanked her, and realized that he still couldn't use the verb *oshieru* properly.

* * *

The verb *oshieru* has several measnings. One is "to teach" as in:

Ima eego-o oshiete-imasu.
(I'm teaching English now.)

Another measning is "to show how to do something" as in:

Eki-e iku michi-o oshiete-kudasai.

12

(please tell me the way to the station.)

When you want to know how to write a kanji, you should say

Kono kanji-no kakikata-o oshiete-kudasai.
(or *Kono kanji-wa doo kakeba ii-deshoo.*)

It can be understood but will sound strange to say *Kono kanji-no kakikata-wa nan-desu-ka.*

When Mr. Lerner said . . . *misete-kudasai*, Miss Yoshida thought he was asking for a booklet or the like because *miseru* usually refers to showing something concrete, as in *hon-o miseru* (to show a book) or *tegami-o miseru* (to show a letter).

A third meaning of *oshieru* is "to give information," corresponding to the English word "tell." For instance when you want to know someone's address or phone number, *oshieru* is usually used as in:

Juusho-o oshiete-kudasai.
(Please tell me your address.)
Denwa-bangoo-o oshiete-kudasaimasen-ka.
電話番号を　教えてくださいませんか。
(Will you please tell me your phone number?)

In these cases too, it sounds awkward to say *Juusho (Denwa-bangoo)-wa nan-desu-ka.*

Kaku yoo-ni iwaremashita
書く ように 言われました
(I was asked to write it)

During lunchtime yesterday. Mr. Lerner was writing a Japanese composition that his Sensee had assigned him as homework. Miss Yoshida came by and asked what he was doing, so he explained that he was writing a composition and added

Sensee-ga tanomimashita-kara.
(Because my teacher asked me to do so.)

Miss Yoshida understood but he felt that his expression was not quite right. He changed it to

Sensee-ni tanomaremashita-kara.
(Because I was asked by my teacher.)

but she didn't seem satisfied. Mr. Lerner then wondered if the verb *tanomu* was wrong in this situation.

*　　　*　　　*

A literal translation of the English sentence "My teacher asked me to write a composition" would be *Sensee-ga sakubun-o kaku koto-o tanomimashita,* but this is not appropriate. The verb *tanomu* is used to mean "to make a request" as in *Yoshida-san-ni shigoto-o tanomimashita* (I asked Miss Yoshida to work for me) or *Kaite kureru yoo-ni tanomimashita* (I asked her to write it for me). But when one tells someone to do what is required as a duty or training, the verb *tanomu* is not used. When a teacher has told his student to write something for practice, one

14

says *Sensee-ga kaku yoo-ni iimashita*; more politely one says . . . *kaku yoo-ni osshaimashita.* Or if the speaker is a student he will often use the passive voice as in

> . . . *kaku yoo-ni iwaremashita.*
> 書く ように 言われました。
> (I was told to write it).

If the teacher's request is made not for the sake of the student but for the teacher himself, *tanomu* is used as in

> *Sensee-ni shigoto-no tetsudai-o tanomaremashita.*
> 先生に 仕事の てつだいを たのまれました。
> (I was asked by my teacher to help him with his work.)

This implies that the teacher has asked the student to do such things as helping make teaching materials or repairing a tape recorder.

In the same way, when a boss tells someone to do something as part of his duties, . . . *yoo-ni yuu* is used, but when he has asked someone to help him personally, *tanomu* is used as in

> *Eego-o oshiete-kureru yoo-ni tanomaremashita.*
> (I was asked to teach him English.)

Mondai-ga arimasu
問題が　あります
(There is a problem)

Mr. Lerner wanted to tell Mr. Mori, the director of the company, that he wanted to be excused
from a meeting scheduled for the next week because his dentist had called him that morning
asking him to change his appointment to the
same afternoon. The situation was rather complicated and Mr. Lerner wasn't sure if he could explain it clearly in Japanese. He started by saying

Mondai-ga arimasu. (There is a problem.)

so that Mr. Mori would be prepared. But Mr.
Mori looked puzzled and a little shocked. While
Mr. Lerner was hurriedly explaining the situation
he looked rather uneasy, but when he understood
he readily said okay. Mr. Lerner wondered how
he should have started his explanation.

*　　　*　　　*

Starting an explanation with *Mondai-ga arimasu* is not appropriate. If someone says it with
a definite tone, the listener will be shocked and
ready to be confronted with a serious difficulty,
because the word *mondai* usually implies a rather
difficult problem. Besides, *mondai-ga aru* is usually used concerning a topic which has already
been brought up as in

Sono hoohoo-niwa mondai-ga arimasu.
(There is a problem with that method.)

And *mondai-ga aru* often implies criticism. If one
says about someone

Mondai-ga atte yameta-soo-desu.

(I understand he quit because he had some problem.)

he implies that the person was involved in something undesirable.

When one wants to explain a situation that needs the listener's judgment or help, one should avoid saying *Mondai-ga arimasu* and use other expressions such as

   . . . no koto-desu-ga . . .
   ……の　ことですが……

and
   . . . no koto-de chotto gosoodan-(or *onegai*)-*shitai-n-desu-ga . . .*

In Mr. Lerner's case above, he might have first said

   Raishuu-no kaigi-no koto-na-n-desu-ga . . .
   来週の　会議の　ことなんですが……
   (This is about the meeting next week but . . .)

to spare Mr. Mori unnecessary apprehension.

And intonation is also important; when one wants to invite the listener's cooperative response, a hesitant, considerate tone will be helpful.

Ii-desu
いいです
(You don't have to)

Mr. Uchida, one of Mr. Lerner's colleagues, had decided to quit the company to study abroad, and Miss Yoshida was busy planning farewell party for him. Mr. Lerner thought he should do something to help her and asked what he could do. She said

Raanaa-san-wa ii-desu.
ラーナーさんは　いいです。

which literally means "You're all right, Mr. Lerner." So he asked again

Watashi-wa nani-ga ii-desu-ka.

to mean "What is a good thing for me to do?" Miss Yoshida looked embarrassed and explained that there were enough people to help her and she knew Mr. Lerner was busy. Finally he understood that she meant "You don't have to do anything" by *ii-desu.*

*　　*　　*

Raanaa-san-wa ii-desu is actually a contraction of . . . *wa tetsudawanakute-mo ii-desu* (You don't have to help me); *tetsudawanakute-mo* is left out because it is obvious. This type of omission is very common in daily conversation. Just as the last part of a phrase like *kaeranakute-wa narimasen* (I have to go home) is often left out, the first part of various phrases can be left out when the meaning is clear.

The phrase preceding *ii-desu* is often left out

when the speaker declines someone's offer or advice. For example:

A: *Ashita mata kimashoo-ka.* (Shall I come again tomorrow?)
B: *Iie, ii-desu.* (No, you don't have to.)

In B's speech, *konakute-mo* is left out before *ii-desu.*

A: *Tsukareta-deshoo. Sukoshi yasundara doo-desu-ka.* (You must be tired. Why don't you rest a while?)
B: *Ii-desu. Moo sukoshi-desu-kara.*
   (No, I don't have to. I can finish it very soon.)

Here *yasumanakute-mo* is left out before *ii-desu.* In such negative answers, *iie* is very often left out, but to say just *ii-desu* can sound abrupt or rude, so a phrase ending in . . . *kara* is often added to avoid sounding rude.

Kekkoo-desu is also used in the same way as *ii-desu* when declining a proposal as in

A: *Moo ippai nomimasen-ka.* (Won't you have another cup?)
B: *Kekkoo-desu.* けっこうです。
   (No, thank you.)

The difference is that *kekkoo* is a little more formal than *ii.*

Kare
かれ
(That fellow)

A few days ago when Mr. Lerner entered the office in the morning, Mr. Takada was talking on the phone. He saw Mr. Lerner coming in and said

Ee, kare-wa ima kimashita.
ええ、かれは　いま　来ました。
(Yes, he has just arrived.)

and called Mr. Lerner to the phone. It was Mr. Okada, and after he had talked with Mr. Lerner, he asked if Mr. Mori, the director, was there. Mr. Lerner answered

Iie, kare-wa kyoo oyasumi-desu.
(No, he is off today.)

After he had finished talking and hung up the phone, Mr. Takada said that he should have said *shachoo* (director) instead of *kare* when referring to Mr. Mori.

After that Mr. Lerner paid special attention to how the Japanese use *kare* and found that it was extremely limited in usage and cannot be considered equivalent to the English "he."

*　　　*　　　*

In daily conversation *kare* or *kanojo* are used to refer to a third person only in very limited situations. First of all, they cannot be used for someone to whom you should refer politely or when you are talking in formal situations; they are used for someone who belongs to the speaker's own group and with whom the speaker is famil-

20

iar. Mr. Mori, for example, is called *shachoo* by his employees, although his intimate friends will call him *kare*.

The use of *kare* or *kanojo* varies widely depending on the speaker. Young people seem to use *kare* and *kanojo* more often than older people, but they also limit it to someone with whom they feel some intimacy.

Another difference from the English "he" and "she" is that *kare* or *kanojo* are used more like a noun, meaning something like "that fellow" or "that girl." Young wives often refer to their husbands with just *kare* in familiar speech as in

Kare-ga matte-ru-kara moo kaeru-wa.

(I'm going home since my husband is waiting for me.)

although they will use *shujin* (my husband) in more formal situations.

Kanojo is also used in a similar way, but it seems to be used in even more limited situations. Among older people, this word often means "a lover" or "a girlfriend." One of our readers who is married to a Japanese man complained that when talking with his parents her husband calls her *Kanojo* instead of using her name. Probably he formed this habit before their marriage when his parents referred to her as *kanojo* and he himself adopted his parents' usage.

Amari osoku naranai uchi-ni
あまり おそく ならない うちに
(Before it becomes very late)

Last Saturday evening Mr. Lerner took Miss Yoshida to a movie. When he went to her house to get her, she was talking with her mother at the door. Her mother asked her what time she would be back. While Miss Yoshida was wondering what time she would be able to come home, her mother said

> *Amari osoku naranai uchi-ni kaette-rasshai.*
> あまり おそく ならない うちに 帰ってらっしゃい。
> (Come home before it's very late.)

Mr. Lerner understood what she had said, but it was difficult for him to recall her sentence word for word. The expression *osoku naranai uchi-ni . . .* seemed very complicated to him; he wondered why she had not simply said *hayaku . . .* (early . . .)

        *   *   *

The word *uchi* literally means "inside" or "within." The expression *. . . nai uchi-ni* means "before . . ."; therefore *osoku naranai uchi-ni* means "before it becomes late," You can also say *osoku naru mae-ni* to mean "before it becomes late," but saying *osoku naranai uchi-ni* implies that the speaker is worried that something undesirable will happen if it becomes late. *. . . nai uchi-ni* is often used when making requests or suggestions as in:

> *Ame-ni naranai uchi-ni kaerimashoo.*
> (Let's go home before it starts raining.)

or
Tsukarenai uchi-ni yametara doo-desu-ka.
(Why don't you stop doing it before you get too tired?)

To say that one should try to cure one's cold before it becomes bad, you can say either *hidoku naru mae-ni* or *hidoku naranai uchi-ni,* but saying

Hidoku naranai uchi-ni naoshita hoo-ga ii-desu-yo.
(It might be better to cure it before it becomes really bad.)

sounds more concerned about the person's health.

Sometimes *uchi-ni* is added to the affirmative form of verbs or adjectives implying "before it becomes otherwise." For instance, *wakai uchi-ni* (while you are young) actually means "before you get too old" as in:

Wakai uchi-ni benkyoo-shita hoo-ga ii.
(You had better study while you're still young.)

Your acquaintances may advise you to do various things
Nihon-ni iru uchi-ni (while you are in Japan) implying "before you have to leave Japan."

Moratte-moraimashita
もらってもらいました
(They kindly received them)

The other day Miss Yoshida said that her cat had had several kittens and wondered if Mr. Takada would like one of them, but he said that his wife didn't like cats very much. After a few days Mr. Takada asked Miss Yoshida what she had done with her kittens. She answered

Tomodachi-ni moratte-moraimashita.
友だちに　もらってもらいました。
(*lit.* I received from my friends the favor of their receiving them.)

Mr. Lerner understood that she had given the kittens to her friends, but wondered if using two *morau*'s as in *moratte-morau* is not strange. He also wondered if she could have said

Tomodachi-ni agemashita.

instead.

*　　　*　　　*

Tomodachi-ni agemashita and *Tomodachi-ni moratte-moraimashita* mean the same thing as far as the facts are concerned, but the speaker's attitude is different. *Tomodachi-ni agemashita* implies that the speaker feels that he has done a favor for his friends, while saying *maratte-morai-mashita* implies that the speaker is thankful to his friends for accepting something.

Needless to say, the same fact can be described differently according to how one feels about it, and in social situations one has to be es-

24

pecially careful about expressions concerning doing or receiving a favor. People often avoid using . . . *te-ageru* because it sounds as if they are emphasizing that they are doing a favor. For instance, when someone is asked to sing a song for others at a party, he will say *Ja, kiite-kudasai* (Well, then, please listen to me), *Ja, kiite-itadaki-mashoo* (Well, then, please listen to me — *lit.* I will receive the favor from you of listening), or *Ja, utawasete-itadakimasu* (*lit.* Then I will receive from you the favor of letting me sing). Saying *Utatte-agemashoo* sounds condescending and as if you are talking to children.

It is polite to describe one's doing a favor as if one is receiving a favor. For instance when one offers help, it is polite to say

   Tetsudawasete-itadakimasu.
   てつだわせていただきます。
   (*lit.* I will receive the favor of letting me help you.)
 or
   Tetsudawasete-kudasai.
   (*lit.* Please allow me to help you.)

rather than saying *Tetsudatte-agemashoo* (*lit.* I will do you the favor of helping you).

Sono kawari
その　かわり
(To make it even)

Mr. Kato, one of Mr. Lerner's colleagues, recently moved to a new apartment house. Yesterday afternoon he was telling Miss Yoshida that his new apartment is located in a very nice, quiet neighborhood. When Miss Yoshida remarked that he was very lucky to find such a good place, Mr. Kato said

Sono kawari, kaisha-kara tooi-n-desu.
その　かわり、会社から　遠いんです。
(*lit.* In its place, it is far from the office.)

Mr. Lerner didn't understand the use of the phrase *sono kawari,* and was wondering what it meant, when Miss Yoshida concluded that everything has two sides, good and bad, and changed the subject.

* * *

Kawari by itself means "substitute" and . . . *no kawari-ni* is used to mean "in place of . . ." or "instead of . . ." as in

Ocha-no kawari-ni koohii-o nomimashita.
(I drank coffee instead of tea.)
Yoshida-san-no kawari-ni watashi-ga iki-mashoo.
(I will go in place of Miss Yoshida.)

In these examples the word *kawari* is used to show a choice between two things. But when it is used together with two contrastive adjectives in decribing something, it does not mean "sub-

26

stitute." For instance, in Mr. Kato's statement, his apartment has two characteristics, being quiet and being far from his office; its being quiet is a merit, but this merit is balanced by a demerit, being far from his office. He could have said this in reverse order too, as in

Kaisha-kara tooi-desu. Sono kawari shizuka-desu.

to mean "It's far from the office. To make up for that, it's quiet." And these two sentences can be put into one as in

Kaisha-kara tooi kawari(-ni) shizuka-desu.
  or
Shizukana kawari(-ni) kaisha-kara tooi-desu.

Thus the expression . . . *no kawari(-ni)* or *sono kawari* is used to connect and balance two things, plus and minus, and make them even.

This expression is also used to show compensation, as in

Kyoo-wa hayaku kaette-mo ii-desu. Sono kawari ashita hayaku kite-kudasai.

(You may leave early today, but please come early tomorrow.)

This means that the speaker wants the listener to make up for leaving early today by coming early tomorrow.

Botsubotsu dekakemashoo-ka
ぼつぼつ　でかけましょうか
(Shall we go out pretty soon?)

Last Saturday afternoon Mr. Lerner went to Professor Takahashi's house to meet him; the professor wanted to take him to an exhibition where some pictures of one of his friends were displayed. The professor asked him to come into the house and have some tea. After they had had the tea, Professor Takahashi said

Ja, botsubotsu dekakemashoo-ka.
じゃ、ぼつぼつ　でかけましょうか。

Mr. Lerner guessed that it meant that it was time to leave, but he didn't understand what *botsubotsu* actually meant.

*　　　*　　　*

The word *botsubotsu* literally means "little by little," and is often used when urging someone to get started as in:

Botsubotsu dekakemashoo-ka. (Shall we go out pretty soon?)
Botsubotsu jikan-desu-ga. (It's about time we started.)

To urge someone to get ready, saying *Botsubotsu . . .* sounds more considerate and polite than saying *Saa, dekakemashoo* (Now let's go out) or *Moo jikan-desu* (It's time now) because *botsubotsu* implies that one can get ready, either emotionally or physically, gradually, without making haste.

It is also used in other situations to mean

"little by little" as in:

A: *Kono-goro doo-desu-ka.*
(How are things these days?)
B: *Maamaa-desu-ne.*
(Oh, so so.)
A: *Seehin, urete-masu-ka.*
(Are your goods selling well?)
B: *Ee, botsubotsu.*
(Yes, they're selling little by little.)

The actual amount of things or speed indicated by *botsubotsu* can be judged only from the context. For example, if you visit someone and he or she is out, and his wife or her husband says

Botsubotsu kaette-kimasu-ga.
(He (She) will be back pretty soon.)

you have to judge whether the person will be back in five minutes or two hours from the way the speaker has said it and from the circumstances. (The word *sorosoro* is also used in a similar way, although it is not used in the case of someone's goods selling little by little.)

Gossori
ごっそり
(In a lot)

Yesterday afternoon Mr. Okada came to the office to see Mr. Lerner and Mr. Takada. Before starting their business discussions, Mr. Lerner asked him if something was wrong because he looked worried. He said that a robber had broken into his house while he was away the previous night. When Mr. Takada asked about the antiques which he had taken so much trouble to collect, he said

Ee, gossori. ええ、ごっそり。

Mr. Lerner understood that Mr. Okada's collection had suffered serious damage, although he didn't know the word *gossori*.

*　　　*　　　*

The adverb *gossori* is used to mean that a large amount of things were stolen or taken away at one time, as in

Hooseki-ga gossori nusumareta.
(The jewels were stolen in their entirety.)
Zeekin-o gossori torareta.
(I had to pay a lot of taxes.)

Very often the verb following an adverb that indicates the manner of action is left out because the meaning is obvious. As in Mr. Okada's answer, a verb such as *toraremashita* (were taken away) or *nusumaremashita* (were stolen) does not have to be added to the word *gossori*. In the same way, when someone asks you

Byooki-wa moo yoku narimashita-ka.
(Have you recovered from your illness?)

you can simply say

Ee, sukkari. ええ、すっかり。
(Yes, completely.)

Or, when asked about your improvement in golf, you can say

Iie, sappari. いいえ、さっぱり。
(No, not at all.)

Sometimes the verb is left out even when there is no preceding question, if the context is provided. In newspaper headlines, for example, verbs are often left out to make the expression short. They will go something like

Bijutsuhin gossori.
(Many pieces of art were stolen.)
Iyana omoide moo sukkari.
(Unpleasant memories have now completely vanished.)
Genzee sappari.
(No signs of tax-reduction can be seen.)

It is helpful to learn adverbs, not by themselves, but together with verbs, so that you can tell what verb has been left out when only an adverb is given.

Kaeranakereba narimasen
帰らなければ　なりません
(I must go home)

Mr. Lerner was invited to a little party at Miss Yoshida's the other day. Staying for some time and having a good time, he thought it was about time to leave. When Miss Yoshida tried to retain him, he said

> *Moo kaeranakereba narimasen.*
> もう　帰らなければ　なりません。
> (I must go home now.)

While the two were talking, Mr. Takada also came to the door and said

> *Boku-mo sorosoro shitsuree-shimasu.*
> ぼくも　そろそろ　失礼します。
> (I'm leaving too, if you don't mind.)

Mr. Lerner then realized that he should have said *Shitsuree-shimasu,* and remembered that Japanese do not usually say *kaeranakereba narimasen* in such situations.

* * *

The expression *kaeranakereba narimasen* is not appropriate when taking leave of someone. In daily conversation such shorter forms as *kaeranakucha* or *kaeranakya* are used in place of *kaeranakereba narimasen.* Sometimes . . . *nakereba narimasen* is used in the middle of a sentence, as in *Haisha-ni ikanakereba narimasen-node . . .* (Since I must go to the dentist . . .), but it is not conversational to end a sentence with . . . *nakereba narimasen.*

The form . . . *nakereba narimasen* is used to end formal, written sentences as in

Kokumin-wa zeekin-o osamenakereba naranai.
(The people must pay taxes.)
Kono daigaku-ni hairu tame-niwa shiken-o uke-nakereba narimasen.
(You have to take an examination to enter this college.)

As seen in these two examples, . . . *nakereba narimasen* is used to state one's duty or require-ments; therefore it is not appropriate for refer-ring to what one wants to do for one's own good or convenience. Saying *Hachiji-made-ni kaeranake-reba narimasen-node* . . . would be all right if the purpose of going home before eight is doing one's work, but it would be strange if the purpose is watching one's favorite situation comedy.

Thus when one is taking his leave from his host's house, one usually avoids using . . . *nake-reba naranai* and chooses such expressions as

Shitsuree-shimasu. (*lit.* I'm going to be rude.)
or
Oitoma-shimasu. (I'm taking my leave.)

Kondo
こんど
(This time)

Mr. Okada came to see Mr. Lerner for a business discussion yesterday afternoon. After commenting on the weather, he said

Kondo hikkosu koto-ni narimashite-ne. . .
こんど 引つ越す ことに なりましてね……
(*lit.* It's decided that I'm going to move this time. . .)

and explained what his new house looked like. While listening to him, Mr. Lerner wondered if the first word *kondo* in Mr. Okada's sentence was really necessary because it did not seem to mean anything in particular.

* * *

The word *kondo* has several usages. One is to mean "this time" in contrast with other times as in

Kondo-wa yoku dekita.
(This time I could do it well.)
Kondo-no hoo-ga yasashii-desu-ne.
(This one is easier.)

Another usage is referring to the future as in

Kondo-wa itsu oide-ni narimasu-ka.
(When will you come next?)

Kondo in Mr. Okada's sentence above is different from these two usages. It is used to indicate that the speaker is going to make an announcement of some significant plan or decision. When a listener hears this word, he prepares himself for an announcement about such things as marriage, change in residence or change in occupation. Most often the announcement concerns what is coming fairly soon as in Mr. Okada's statement, and the sentence is often concluded with . . . *koto-ni narimashita* or . . . *koto-ni shimashita* as in

Kondo kekkon-suru koto-ni narimashita.
(*lit.* It's decided that I'm going to get married.)
Kondo kaisha-o yameru koto-ni shimashita.
(I have decided to quit the company.)

The announcement can be about what has already happened as in

Kondo kisoku-ga kawarimashita.
(The regulation has been revised.)

And on formal occasions *kono tabi* is used in place of *kondo* as in

Kono tabi-wa ojoosama-ga kekkon-nasaru soo-de . . .
この　たびは　おじょうさまが　結婚なさる
そうで……
(I heard that your daughter is going to get married.)

Hora
ほら
(Look!)

Miss Yoshida brings Mr. Lerner's mail to him every day around 11 o'clock. She usually says while handing it to him

Hai, yuubin-desu.
はい、郵便です。
(Here's your mail.)

But this morning she had more letters than usual, and said

Hora, konna-ni takusan kimashita.
ほら、こんなに　たくさん　来ました。
(Look, this many letters came!)

While thanking her, Mr. Lerner wondered if he had ever heard this word *hora* before.

*　　　*　　　*

The word *hai* has various usages. It is used as an affirmative to mean "yes, that's right"; it is used as *aizuchi* to mean "I understood what you said"; it is also used to show finality as in *Wakarimashita, hai* (Yes, yes, I understand). It is also used, as in Miss Yoshida's case, when handing something to others as in

Hai, otsuri-desu. (Here's your change.)
Hai, uketori-desu. (Here's your receipt.)

or simply *Hai* or *Hai, doozo* to mean "Here you are."

This *hai* indicates that some action, for instance, handing something to others, has been completed, and urges the listener to act accordingly. It is also used to mean that the speaker has completed some preparations and wants the listener to make use of them. For instance, when someone gets the taperecorder ready for you, he will say

> *Hai, yooi-ga dekimashita.*

so that you can start recording.

On the other hand, *hora* is used to call someone's attention to some situation or to what has happened, as in

> *Hora, asoko-ni suzume-ga tomatte-imasu.*
> (Look! There are some sparrows over there.)
> *Hora, henna oto-ga suru-deshoo?*
> (Listen, don't you hear that strange sound?)

So, when Miss Yoshida said, *Hora, konna-ni takusan kimashita,* she wanted Mr. Lerner to pay attention to the quantity of the mail, while when she says *Hai, yuubin-desu,* she simply wants him to accept the mail and take care of it.

Guchi-o yuu
ぐちを 言う
(To complain)

The other day when Mr. Lerner met Mr. Okada after not having seen him for some time, he thought he looked very tired. Mr. Okada said that someone who had been helping him had suddenly left the company so he was quite busy. When Mr. Lerner asked if the company director was not going to find someone else to help him, he said that the director was not very considerate of him. Mr. Lerner felt sorry for him and wondered if there was anything he could do to help him. Then Mr. Okada looked surprised and told him to forget about it, saying

Guchi-o itta dake-desu-kara.
ぐちを 言った だけですから。

Mr. Lerner understood that this meant "I was only complaining," but he didn't understand what was implied by *guchi-o itta.*

*   *   *

Guchi-o yuu or *guchi-o kobosu* refers to complaining, usually not to the person who has caused the trouble, but to someone who will listen to the speaker and sympathize with him. In other words, when a person says *guchi,* he usually doesn't expect the listener to start any action to solve the problem. What counts is the satisfaction obtained by having an outlet for one's dissatisfaction and being comforted by the listener's sympathy.

Sometimes *kobosu* (こぼす) alone can stand for *guchi-o kobosu,* as in

Kyoo-wa Okada-san, daibu koboshite-ikima-shita-ne.

(Mr. Okada complained a lot today.)

Okada-san-ni kobosarete komarimashita.

(Mr. Okada complained so much that I was embarrassed. — *lit.* I was complained by Mr. Okada so much that I was at a loss.)

When people gather and talk together at bars or restaurants after the day's work, they often complain. They will grumble that they are not paid well enough and that they have to work for bosses who lack any kindness or understanding. When they complain about these things over a cup or coffee or a glass of beer, they usually don't expect their listeners to do something about these problems the next day. This is a typical case of *guchi-o yuu* or *guchi-o kobosu*. And the listeners usually listen to their companions' *guchi* with enthusiastic *aizuchi* (reply words) and expressions of their sympathy.

Doo shita mon-deshoo-ne
どう した もんでしょうね
(I wonder what should be done about it)

Mr. Lerner was impressed by the patience with which Mr. Takada had listened to Mr. Okada grumbling about his boss. He thought that he should also become a good listener to maintain good relations with the Japanese around him, so he decided to observe closely how Mr. Takada and others listen to someone's complaints. He found that the phrases most often used are ones such as *Taihen-desu-ne* (That's tough) and *Komarimashita-ne* (It's quite troubling, isn't it?). Just yesterday he was surprised to hear Mr. Takada say

> *Doo shita mon-deshoo-ne.*
> どう した もんでしょうね。
> (I wonder what should be done about it.)

as if he himself were complaining.

* * *

When someone says *guchi* (complains), he usually expects the listener to sympathize with him. These expressions of sympathy must sound like the two people, complainer and sympathizer, share the same feelings and the same standpoint.

Saying that you understand the situation or that you agree with the complainer is not very appropriate as an expression of sympathy because it implies that you are in a different position from the complainer.

Thus the sympathizer will say just what the complainer would say. For instance, when the complainer says that his boss is unkind, the sympathizer will say something like

Taihen-desu-ne.

And when the complainer describes a difficult situation he is in, the sympathizer will say

Komarimashita-ne.

as if he himself were in the difficult situation.

Sometimes the sympathizer will go so far as to feel vexed by the difficult situation the complainer is in and wonder what could be done about it. Thus Mr. Takada said

Doo shita mon-deshoo-ne.

to express his sympathy, just as many other Japanese would do.

Mite-kimashita
見てきました
(I saw them)

During lunchtime yesterday, someone started talking about an exhibition of the works of a famous Spanish painter. When Miss Yoshida asked the people there if they had seen it, Mr. Lerner said

Ee, mimashita. (Yes, I saw it.)

but Mr. Takada and several others said

Boku-mo mite-kimashita.
ぼくも　見てきました。

Mr. Lerner wondered why they had added *ki-mashita* instead of simply saying *mimashita.* If it was about something they had done immediately before and then come back to the office, he could understand it, but this was about something they had done several days before, so Mr. Lerner found it strange.

*　　*　　*

. . . *te-kuru* is used to imply that the speaker did something and then came to the listener. When one says *Tenrankai-o mimashita* (I saw the exhibition), he is just referring to the fact that he saw the exhibition, and he is not concerned about the fact that he is now with the listener. On the other hand, when one says *Mite-kimashita,* he implies that he saw it and is now with the listener. In other words, . . . *te-kuru* emphasizes that the speaker is concerned with the existence of the listener.

42

When two friends or acquaintances talk about their respective experiences, they often use the . . . *te-kuru* form as in

Senshuu Fuji-san-ni nobotte-kimashita.
(I went and climbed Mount Fuji last week.)
Kono-aida-no soobetsukai, boku itte-kita-yo.
(I went to the farewell party the other day.)

Usually these sentences are followed by further discussion of their experiences, because the . . . *te-kuru* form implies that the speaker wants the listener to share his experience more fully.

For this reason the form . . . *te-kuru* can be used to build up a familiar atmosphere. For instance, when starting a public speech, rather than saying *Senjitsu Chuugoku-e ikimashita,* a speaker will often say to the audience

Senjitsu Chuugoku-e itte-kimashita.
先日　中国へ　行ってきました。

to mean "I went to China the other day," because this implies that the speaker feels he belongs to the same group as the audience and is eager to share his experience with them.

Joozu-ni natte-ikimashita
じょうずに なっていきました
(It kept on improving)

Mr. Lerner noticed that Miss Yoshida's English had improved quite rapidly, so he remarked to Mr. Takada the other day

Yoshida-san-no eego-wa joozu-ni natte-iki-mashita-ne.

meaning "Miss Yoshida's English has improved." Mr. Takada agreed, but corrected his sentence to

. . . joozu-ni natte-kimashita.
じょうずに なってきました。

Mr. Lerner had thought that both . . . *te-iku* and . . . *te-kuru* were used to mean "keep . . . ing," and had not learned the difference between the two.

* * *

While . . . *te-kuru* is used to refer to an action approaching the speaker, . . . *te-iku* refers to an action going away from him. Therefore, a change up to the present is usually described with . . . *te-kuru* as in

Samuku natte-kimashita.
さむく なってきました。
(It has become cold.)
Eego-ga joozu-ni natte-kimashita. (Her English has improved.)
Bukka-ga agatte-kimashita. (Things have become more expensive.)

44

And . . . *te-iku* is used most often to refer to a change continuing into the future as in

Kore-kara samuku natte-ikimasu.
これから　さむく　なっていきます。
(It will become colder from now on.)
Bukka-ga agatte-iku-deshoo.
(Things will become more and more expensive.)

Since . . . *te-iku* implies that an action or state of things is going away from the speaker, it is appropriate to use it to refer to the future in conversation, but it is also used to refer to the past in written sentences where the writer is supposed to be detached from the action or the state of things that he is writing about. For instance, to describe how Japan was modernized in the Meiji Period;

Nihon-wa kooshite shidai-ni kindaika-shite-itta.
(In this way Japan was gradually modernized.)

Or, referring to the hero of his novel, an author may write

Kare-wa sono kesshin-o tsuyomete-itta.
(He was more and more determined to do so.)

This use of . . . *te-iku* is often seen in textbooks or literary writings because it implies the detached attitude of the writer.

Shinbun-ni yoru-to
新聞に よると
(According to the newspaper)

Yesterday morning Mr. Lerner read in the newspaper that two people had died of shock in the earthquake the night before. He wanted to talk about this news to Miss Yoshida, and started saying

Shinbun-ni yotte . . .

to mean "According to the newspaper," and wondered if he was right. Then Miss Yoshida said

"Shinbun-ni yoru-to"-deshoo?
(You mean "Shinbun-ni yoru-to"?)

and smiled. He remembered that he had made the same mistake before, perhaps more than once.

*   *   *

While . . . *ni yotte* is used to show the means to do something, . . . *ni yoru-to* is used to show the source of information as in

Shinbun-ni yoru-to yuube-no jishin-wa kanari ookikatta-soo-desu.
新聞に よると ゆうべの 地震は かなり

大きかったそうです。
(According to the newspaper, the earthquake last night was quite big.)
    or
Shushoo-no hanashi-ni yoru-to, genzee-wa shinai-soo-desu.
(According to the prime minister's state-

ment, taxes will not be reduced.)

To show a source of information, however, several other expressions are used rather than . . . *ni-yoru-to*, which sounds formal; the following expressions are used in daily conversation:

Shinbun-ni kaite-atta-n-desu-ga . . .
(It was written in the newspaper that . . .)
Shinbun-de yonda-n-desu-ga . . .
(I read in the newspaper that . . .)
Terebi-no nyuusu-de itte-imashita-ga . . .
(They said on the TV news that . . .)

And when conveying someone's statement, it is more conversational to say *Yamamoto-san-ga itte-ta-n-desu-ga . . .* or *Yamamoto-san-ni kiita-n-desu-ga . . .* than saying *Yamamoto-san-no hanashi-ni yoru-to . . .*

Ima-goro
いまごろ
(At this time)

Yesterday afternoon Mr. Okada came for business discussions with Mr. Lerner and Mr. Takada. Before starting their discussions, Mr. Okada asked Mr. Lerner how his parents were. Mr. Lerner said that they must be all right because he hadn't heard from them recently, and added that he himself hadn't written to them for some time because

Ima-goro isogashikute.

meaning "I am busy these days." Then Mr. Takada corrected his expression to *Kono-goro* . . . But then when Mr. Okada mentioned that his parents lived in Hokkaido, Mr. Takada himself said

Ima-goro-wa samukute taihen-deshoo.
いまごろは　さむくて　たいへんでしょう。
(It must be tough for them because it's so cold there at this time.)

Mr. Lerner wondered what difference there was between *ima-goro* and *kono-goro*; didn't they both mean "these days"?

*　　*　　*

Kono-goro refers to the present situation where the speaker himself is involved. Therefore one usually says

Kono-goro-wa samui hi-ga ooi-desu-ne.
このごろは　さむい　日が　多いですね。

48

(We are having many cold days now.)
Kono-goro doomo tsukareyasukute . . .
(I get tired easily these days.)

Or, even when talking about someone else, *kono-goro* is used if the person is included in the same situation as the speaker, as in

Ano-hito-wa kono-goro genki-ga arimasen-ne.
(He doesn't look very well these days.)

On the other hand, *ima-goro* is used to refer to the present time in general, when the speaker is not particularly included in the situation.
Thus one often says

Ano-hito-wa ima-goro doo shite-iru-deshoo.
(I wonder what he is doing now.)
Ima-goro futari-ni akachan-ga umarete-iru-deshoo.
(They must have had a baby by this time.)

Ima-goro is also used to mean "at this time of the year" as in

Mainon ima-goro-wa yuki-ga ooi.
(It always snows a lot at this time of the year.)

And *mainen* can be left out when it is understood. Thus when Mr. Takada said *Ima-goro-wa samu-kute taihen-deshoo* about Mr. Okada's parents, he used the phrase *ima-goro* in the sense of "at this time of the year."

Oboete-imasen
おぼえていません
(I don't remember)

Mr. Lerner was talking about a movie that had been popular recently, but couldn't remember the name of the heroine, so he turned to Miss Yoshida for help saying

Yoshida-san, oboemasen-ka.

meaning "Don't you remember it, Miss Yoshida?" She didn't answer for a moment, and then said *Saa, nan-te itta-kashira* (Well, I wonder what her name was), and finally said *Watashi-mo oboete-imasen* (I don't remember, either). Mr. Lerner realized then that he should have asked *oboete-imasen-ka* instead of *oboemasen-ka,* but he still couldn't help wondering how *oboeru* and *oboete-iru* are so different.

*   *   *

While *oboete-iru* means "to remember," *oboeru* does not mean "remember" at all. It implies an effort to learn something and memorize it, as in

Kanji-o oboeru-no-wa taihen-desu.
(It is a lot of work to learn kanji.)
Nakanaka oboeraremasen.
(It is very difficult for me to memorize it.)

On the other hand, *oboete-iru* refers to the action of keeping something in one's memory, as in

Sore-wa mada oboete-imasu.
それは　まだ　おぼえています。

(I still remember that.)
Komakai koto-wa oboete-imasen.
こまかい　ことは　おぼえていません。
(I don't remember the details.)

Thus, the two forms of the verb *oboeru* should be considered as having two different meanings — "to memorize" and "to remember."

But to refer to something not in one's memory, several expressions other than *oboete-iru* are very often used in daily conversation. When asked to recall someone's name, for instance, and unable to do so, one often says

Saa, nan-te itta-deshoo.
(Well, I wonder what his name was.)
Nan-to yuu namae-deshita-kke.
(I wonder what his name was.)
  or
Wasuremashita.
(I forget.)

And when asking someone to remember something, one usually says

Wasurenaide-kudasai.
(Please don't forget it.)

rather than *oboete-ite-kudasai*. This is true of remembering to do something, too. To ask someone to remember to mail a letter, one usually says

Yuubin-o dasu-noo wasurenaide-kudasai.
(Please don't forget to mail the letter.)

Tsumori
つもり
(Intention)

The other day Mr. Lerner noticed that Miss Yoshida was looking for something. When he asked her about it, she answered that she was looking for a copy of a letter, and added, pointing to the desk

Koko-ni oita tsumori-na-n-desu-kedo.
ここに　おいた　つもりなんですけど。

Mr. Lerner understood that she thought she had left it on the desk, but he didn't understand why she had used the word *tsumori*. He had learned that *tsumori* was used to express one's intention as in *Dekakeru tsumori-desu* (I intend to go out), so he wondered how it could be used with the past form of a verb as in *oita tsumori*.

*　　　*　　　*

When *tsumori* follows the present form of a verb, it describes one's intentions. But when it follows the past form of a verb, it expresses a person's beliefs as in

Koko-ni oita tsumori-desu.
(I think I put it here.)
Dekiru dake-no koto-wa shita tsumori-desu.
(I believe that I have done all I can.)

When compared with . . . *to omoimasu* (I think that . . .), this use of *tsumori* implies that the speaker is eager to assert himself. *Dekiru dake-no koto-wa shita tsumori-desu* is often said to defend oneself when blamed for something.

Sometimes the present form of a verb can also be used with *tsumori* in this sense, if the verb describes a state rather than an action, as in

Sono kurai-wa wakaru tsumori-desu.
(I think I can understand that much.)

which implies "so you don't have to tell me."

Adjectives are also used with *tsumori* to reflect the belief or self-assertion of the speaker as in

Watashi-wa mada wakai tsumori-desu-ga.
わたしは まだ わかい つもりですが。
(I think I am still young.)

When *tsumori* is used in this way with the second or third person, the speaker is usually being sarcastic about the person's belief. For instance, saying *Ano-hito-wa wakai tsumori-desu* implies that everyone else thinks otherwise.

Itsu okaeshi-sureba yoroshii-deshoo
いつ おかえしすれば よろしいでしょう
(When would you like me to return it?)

Mr. Mori, the director of the company, has a fine collection of woodblock prints, and Mr. Lerner wanted to borrow some of them for a few days. He asked Mr. Mori

Itsu kaeshite-moraitai-desu-ka.

to mean "When would you like me to return them?" Mr. Mori didn't answer for a moment, and then said he would like to have them back within a week. When Mr. Lerner told Miss Yoshida about this, she said that he should have said

Itsu okaeshi-sureba yoroshii-deshoo.
いつ おかえしすれば よろしいでしょう。
(*lit.* When will it be all right for me to return them?)

instead. Mr. Lerner wondered if there was no expression in Japanese corresponding to the English "Would you like me to . . . ?"

* * *

To politely ask someone's wishes, the form . . . *tai-desu-ka* or . . . *te-moraitai-desu-ka* should be avoided, because . . . *tai* does not express politeness and is mainly used with the first person or with the second person when one does not have to be polite.

One usually asks someone's wishes politely with . . . *shimashoo-ka* or . . . *sureba yoroshii-deshoo*; in both cases the subject of the sentence is the speaker, as in

Kono tsugi-wa itsu ukagai-(or *mairi-*)*mashoo-ka.*
(When should I come next time?)
Kono tsugi-wa itsu ukagaeba yoroshii-deshoo.
この つぎは いつ うかがえば よろしいでしょう。
(When should I come next time?)

(*Maireba* sounds old-fashioned.)
To ask someone politely ''When would you like to have it?'' there are such expressions as

Itsu motte-kureba yoroshii-deshoo. (*lit.* When will it be all right for me to bring it?)
Itsu motte-agareba yoroshii-deshoo. (The same as above, but this sounds more humble.)
Itsu owatashi-sureba yoroshii-deshoo. (*lit.* When will it be good for me to hand it over to you?)

Saying *Itsu tsukaitai-desu-ka* (When do you want to use it?) or *Itsu hoshii-desu-ka* (When do you want it?) sounds blunt and awkward. It is better to use such expressions as

Itsu oiriyoo-desu-ka.
(When would be needing it?)
Itsu otsukai-ni narimasu-ka.
(When would be using it?)

Tsuide-ni
ついでに
(While. . .)

Yesterday afternoon Miss Yoshida told Mr. Lerner and Mr. Takada that she was going to the post office and asked if they wanted her to buy anything for them. Then Mr. Takada said

Ja, Tsuide-ni tabako katte-kite-kudasai.
じゃ、ついでに　たばこ　買ってきてください。
(Then will you buy me some cigarettes on the way?)

Mr. Lerner realized that he had once learned the expression *tsuide-ni* and had heard it used many times, but that he had never used it himself. He knew that *tsuide-ni* refers to doing something while doing something else, as buying cigarettes while going to the post office, but he was not sure which action should be done first or whether the order didn't matter.

*　　*　　*

The word *tsuide* fundamentally means "next" or "of second importance"; *tsuide-ni . . . suru* means "to do something of second importance, taking advantage of a chance to do something." For instance, in Miss Yoshida's case, going to the post office is the business of the first importance for her, and buying cigarettes for Mr. Takada is second in importance. It does not matter whether she buys the cigarettes on her way to the post office or on her way back; what matters is which action is more important.

This expression *tsuide-ni* is often used when asking someone to do a favor in a reserved way;

it is considerate to assume that one's request should not be regarded as first in importance. Thus, one often uses this expression to ask a person going out on business to do something, as in

Tsuide-ni kono tegami dashite-kudasai.
(Please mail this letter for me while you're out.)

Sometimes *tsuide-ga attara* (*lit.* if you have a chance to do something of second importance) or *tsuide-no toki-ni* (*lit.* when you have a chance to do something of second importance) is used in social situations when asking a favor to show one's reserve, as in

A: *Itsu okaeshi-sureba yoroshii-deshoo.*
(When would you like me to return it?)
B: *Ie, itsu-demo kekkoo-desu.*
(Any time will do.)
A: *Soo-desu-ka. Demo . . .*
(Well, . . .)
B: *Itsuka otsuide-no toki-ni omochi-kudasai.*
いつか おついでの ときに お持ちください。
(Please bring it when you happen to come by.)

This implies that the listener does not have to come for that purpose alone (*wazawaza*), but that he can bring it when he is visiting the speaker for some other purpose.

Sono-uchi
その うち
(By and by)

Mr. Okada came to discuss some business with Mr. Lerner the other day, and when he was leaving after the discussions, he said he had something to ask Miss Yoshida, but she had just stepped out of the office. Mr. Lerner suggested that Mr. Okada have a cup of coffee and wait for her, adding

Chikai uchi-ni modotte-kimasu-kara.

meaning "Because she will be back very soon." Mr. Okada agreed, saying

Ee, sono-uchi mieru-deshoo.
ええ、そのうち　みえるでしょう。
(Yes, she will show up pretty soon.)

Mr. Lerner wondered if he was wrong when he said *chikai uchi-ni*; he had learned that *uchi* is used to refer to a time interval, and he thought that both *chikai uchi-ni* and *sono uchi-ni* meant "before long," but he didn't know the difference between the two.

*　　　*　　　*

Mr. Lerner's sentence sounded strange because *chikai uchi-ni* cannot be used to refer to something that will happen during the same day. Although it does not specify the time, it usually refers to things that are likely to take place after a few days or after a few weeks or months, and not after a few minutes.

On the other hand, *sono-uchi(-ni)* is used to refer more indefinitely to the future. It can be used for what will happen after a few minutes as in Mr. Okada's remark about Miss Yoshida's coming back. It is also used to refer to what will happen after a fairly long time as in

> *Sono uchi-ni keeki-mo kaifuku-suru-deshoo.*
> (Business will improve one of these days.)

Because of this indefiniteness, *sono uchi(-ni)* is often used in social situations as in

A: *Doozo ichido oasobi-ni oide-kudasai.*
どうぞ いちど おあそびに おいでください。
(Please come to see us.)
B: *Arigatoo-gozaimasu. Izure sono-uchi-ni.*
ありがとうございます。いずれ そのうちに。
(Thank you. I will come sometime.)

Hachiji-ni naranakereba kaerimasen
八時に　ならなければ　帰りません
(He won't be back before eight)

The other day Mr. Lerner happened to pass by Professor Takahashi's house and dropped in to see if he was home. The professor was not home, but Mrs. Takahashi asked him to come in. After talking a while he asked her what time the professor would be back. Then she looked a little embarrassed and answered hesitantly

Hachiji-ni naranakereba kaerimasen-kedo . . .
八時に　ならなければ　帰りませんけど……
(*lit.* He won't be back if it does not become eight, but . . .)

Mr. Lerner thanked her for the tea and left. He wondered why she had used a double negative instead of simply saying

Hachiji-ni kaerimasu.
(He will be back at eight.)

And he also remembered that he had come across this type of double negative very often, but that he himself hadn't used it very much.

*　　*　　*

Double negatives such as *Hachiji-ni naranakereba kaerimasen* or *Ashita-de nakereba dekimasen* (It won't be ready before tomorrow) are used to emphasize the condition; for example, in *Hachiji-ni naranakereba kaerimasen,* the condition that it has to be eight is emphasized.

Replying to the question "When can you leave your office in the evening?" with

Rokuji-ni naranakereba deraremasen.
六時に　ならなければ　出られません。
(I can't leave the office before six.)

reflects the speaker's feelings about his having to stay until six, whether it be irritation or pride in being an important person.

In Mrs. Takahashi's case mentioned above, she used a double negative in order to imply that she was sorry about Mr. Lerner's having to wait a long time for Professor Takahashi. Saying *Hachiji-ni kaerimasu* would have sounded matter-of-fact and impersonal, as if she were not concerned at all about Mr. Lerner's feelings.

Osaki-ni
お先に
(Excuse me)

Mr. Lerner was invited to a little party at Miss Yoshida's last Saturday, and had a very good time. Mr. Takada was also invited, but he left early, saying that he had to take care of his sick wife. When he was leaving he said

Osaki-ni shitsuree-shimasu.
お先に　失礼します。
(*lit.* I'm going to be rude and leave before you.)

Mr. Lerner remembered that people usually say *Osaki-ni* when leaving the office before others; he had thought that it had to be said because the speaker was leaving when others had to work. He wondered why it has to be said when leaving a party, too. The one leaving early is going to miss the fun, and why does he have to apologize for it? Is it because his absence is going to affect the other people's fun?

*　　*　　*

Osaki-ni by itself can mean either "before you" or "after you." When one says *Doozo osaki-ni* to someone at the entrance of a building or room, for example, it means "Please go ahead" or "After you." In this case, *doozo* is usually added either before or after the phrase.

On the other hand, when one says *Osaki-ni* before doing something, like leaving or helping oneself to food or entering the bath, he means "Excuse me" or "Excuse me for going ahead of you." In this case *shitsuree-shimasu* is either said verbally or understood after the phrase.

If one belongs to the group, it is appropriate to say *Osaki-ni* or *Osaki-ni shitsuree-shimasu* when leaving the others, whether they may be working or having fun. Saying *Kaerimasu* (I'm going home) or *Ikanakereba narimasen* (I must go) does not sound appropriate in social situations.

This expression is said not only to one's superiors but also to one's equals or to younger members of the group. The underlying idea for this is that a member of a group is supposed to feel guilty in breaking away from the others and by doing so affecting the unity of the group. It seems that many Japanese regard it as important for a group member to be together with the others, not only emotionally but also physically, both in work and in fun.

Takaku natta mon-desu-ne
高く なった もんですね
(It certainly has become expensive)

Mr. Lerner and Mr. Takada had some *soba* for lunch yesterday. When they paid the bill, they were a little surprised that the price had been raised again. After they left the shop, Mr. Lerner said

Takaku narimashita-ne.
(It has become very expensive, hasn't it?)

Then Mr. Takada agreed, saying

Soo-desu-ne. Soba-mo takaku natta mon-desu-ne.

Mr. Lerner understood that Mr. Takada had agreed with him, and he remembered that he had heard the expression . . . *mon-desu-ne* used very often, but he had not used it much himself. He wondered what difference there was between *takaku narimashita* and *takaku natta mon-desu-ne.*

* * *

The word *mono* or *mon* is used to refer not only to concrete things but also to facts or situations. When *mon-desu* or *mono-desu* is added to a sentence, it implies that the speaker is referring to a thing or fact after having given it deep, even philosophical, thought. Mr. Takada could have said *Takaku narimashita-ne,* too, but when he said *Takaku natta mon-desu-ne,* he implied that he had thought about the fact deeply and was strongly agreeing with Mr. Lerner.

This expression is used very often when stating one's impression about some fact or situation. For instance, when one hears about someone's sudden death he will say

Ningen-te wakaranai mon-desu-ne.
(It is not ours to tell what will become of us.)

Or, when one is surprised at a change in society, he will say

Yo-no-naka-mo kawatta mon-desu-ne.
世の中も　変わった　もんですね。
(Things have certainly changed.)

This is also used when reflecting on what happened in the past. Compared with saying *Ano koro-wa yoku hatarakimashita* (I worked hard those days), saying

Ano koro-wa yoku hataraita mon-desu.
あの　ころは　よく　働いた　もんです。

implies that the speaker is looking back on those days with deep emotion, whether it be pity or admiration for himself.

Nande mata sonna koto-o . . .
なんで　また　そんな　ことを……
(Why on earth are you doing
such a thing?)

Yesterday evening after work was over, Mr. Lerner and Mr. Takada asked Miss Yoshida to go out and have some tea with them, but Miss Yoshida said that she was going to school. When Mr. Takada asked her what she was studying, she said her class was in how to wear kimono. Mr. Takada looked surprised and said

Nande mata sonna koto-o narau-no.
なんで　また　そんな　ことを　習うの。
(*lit.* Why are you studying such a thing again?)

Mr. Lerner wondered why Mr. Takada had used *mata,* which he understood meant "again." Miss Yoshida was learning it for the first time, wasn't she?

*　　　*　　　*

Mata is used to mean "again" as in

Mata oide-kudasai. (Please come again.)
Mata machigaeta. (I made a mistake again.)

Or, when departing, one often says

Mata ashita. (See you tomorrow.)
 or
Mata raishuu. (See you next week.)

However, this *mata* is sometimes used in a different sense. When Mr. Takada said *Nande mata sonna koto-o narau-no, mata* is used to emphasize his surprise. He actually meant "Why on earth are you studying such a thing?" *Mata* is used with expressions of surprise as in

Kore-wa mata mezurashii tokoro-de ome-ni kakarimashita-ne.

(I never expected to run into you here.)

Dooshite mata kyuu-ni yametaku natta-n-desu-ka.

(How come you want to quit all of a sudden?)

When *mata* is used to express surprise in this way, the rest of the sentence can be understood without being said. Mr. Takada could have just said

Nande mata sonna koto-o . . .

or even

Nande mata . . .

Yasumi-tte ii mon-desu-ne
休みって いい もんですね
(Holidays are certainly nice, aren't they?)

Mr. Takada had a few days off to visit his parents in the country and came back to the office yesterday. When Mr. Lerner asked him about his vacation, he answered that it had done him a lot of good, and added

Yasumi-tte honto-ni ii mon-desu-ne.
休みって ほんとに いい もんですね。
(Holidays are certainly nice, aren't they?)

Mr. Lerner did not understand this at first, because he failed to hear the first phrase *Yasumi-tte.* He could just hear *mitte,* and was wondering what it meant, when Miss Yoshida said, *Watashi-mo yasumi-ga hoshii-wa* (I want some holidays, too). So Mr. Lerner realized that Mr. Takada had said *Yasumi-tte* instead of *mitte,* and he remembered that he had long been troubled by this *-tte* sound.

*   *   *

-tte stands for *to, to yuu, to yuu mono-wa* or *to yuu-no-wa.* The particle *to* used to indicate a quoted statement is often pronounced *-tte* as in

Kyoo-wa konai-tte iimashita.
(He said that he is not coming today.)

And *iimashita* and such other verbs are often left out as in *Kyoo-wa konai-tte*

-tte is used to mean *to yuu* in the following sentences.

Yamada-tte hito-ga kimashita.
(A person called Yamada came.)
Yasumu-tte koto-wa taisetsu-desu.
(Taking a rest is important.)

And in Mr. Takada's statement above, *-tte* stands for *to yuu mono-wa* which emphasizes the subject matter; *Yasumi-tte* stands for *Yasumi-to yuu mono-wa*. *-tte* is used in the same way in the following sentences.

Yo-no-naka-tte wakaranai mon-desu-ne.
世の中って わからない もんですね。
(It is hard to tell what will happen in this world.)
Nihongo-tte muzukashii-desu-ne.
(The Japanese language is difficult.)

-tte is also used to ask for explanation as in

A: *Eki-no soba-desu.* (It's near the station.)
B: *Eki-tte doko-no-desu-ka.* (Which station?)

In this case *-tte* stands for *to yuu-no-wa.*
-tte is certainly used in many ways — *-tte muzukashii-desu-ne.*

Komarimasu-ne, ano-hito
こまりますね、あの人
(He's certainly annoying, isn't he?)

While having tea after lunch yesterday, Miss Yoshida complained about one of their colleagues who was not very cooperative, Mr. Kato. She said with a sigh

Komarimasu-ne, ano-hito.
こまりますね、あの人。

Mr. Lerner thought that this meant "He is in trouble," and wondered why she said so; wasn't it Miss Yoshida rather than Mr. Kato that was annoyed? Then Mr. Takada said

Komaru-yone, minna.
(He certainly annoys everyone, doesn't he?)

Upon hearing this, Mr. Lerner realized that by *Komarimasu-ne* Miss Yoshida was referring to herself rather than *ano-hito*.

* * *

The verb *komaru* by itself means "to be annoyed" or "to be troubled." When it is used without mentioning the subject, as in *Komarimasu-ne*, it usually refers to the speaker's being annoyed. If the speaker is annoyed by someone else, he says

Ano-hito-niwa komarimasu.
(I'm annoyed by him.)

The *ni* in this sentence is often left out as in *Ano-hito-wa komarimasu*, and even *wa* can be left out as in *Ano-hito, komarimasu* or *Komarimasu, ano-hito*.

But *Ano-hito(-wa) komarimasu* can refer to the third person depending upon the context as in:

A: *Ano-hito daijoobu-deshoo-ka.*
   (Do you think he will be all right?)
B: *Saa, okane-ga nakunaru-to komarimasu-ne.*
   (Well, he will be in trouble if his money runs out.)

And *komatte-iru* can be used with any person as in
I. A: *Ano-hito kono-goro doo-desu-ka.*
      (How is he these days?)
   B: *Daibu komatte-iru yoo-desu-yo.*
      (He seems to be in quite a bit of trouble.)
II. A: *Kono-goro doo-desu-ka.*
       (How are you doing these days?)
    B: *Dare-mo kyooryoku-shite-kurenai-n-de ko-matte-imasu.*
       (No one cooperates with me, so I'm troubled.)

Komatta also refers to the speaker as well as others as in
Komatta toki-wa enryo naku kite-kudasai.
(Please feel free to come to me if you're in trouble.)
Ano-hito, komatta mon-desu-ne.
(He's certainly annoying, isn't he?)

In fact, who is troubled is made clear by expressions indicating the relationship between the speaker and the third person and by the context.

71

Isogashii-ttara nai-n-desu
いそがしいったら　ないんです
(I'm too busy for words)

Yesterday afternoon when Mr. Lerner was walking back to the office after lunch he ran into Mr. Sakai, a worker at a nearby company. When Mr. Lerner asked him how he was, he said

Isogashii-ttara nai-n-desu-yo.
いそがしいったら　ないんですよ。

Mr. Lerner just heard the words *isogashii* (busy) and *nai* (not), and wondered if Mr. Sakai was busy or not, but since he looked busy, he used the common expression which seemed to be appropriate

Taihen-desu-ne. (That's tough.)
　　　　　*　　　　*　　　　*

Mr. Lerner said the right thing because Mr. Sakai actually meant "I am too busy for words." *Isogashii-ttara nai* literally means "If you talk about being busy, there are no words to describe it." In the same way

Samui-ttara nai.
さむいったら　ない。

means "It's too cold for words." or "It's indescribably cold." Saying

Kuyashii-ttara nai.

means "It's so vexing."
Sometimes nouns are used before *-ttara* as in

72

Ano-hito-no kao-ttara nakatta.
(How he looked is beyond expression.)
Kinoo-no samusa-ttara nakatta.
(It was indescribably cold yesterday.)

-ttara is used to emphasize the subject as in

Ano-hito-ttara komaru-n-desu-yo.
(As for that person he's quite annoying.)

-ttara and *-tte* are similar in that both of them are used to emphatically indicate the subject, but the difference is that *-ttara* is used for what the speaker has a special feeling about or what he evaluates, mostly negatively. Therefore you can say

Raishuu-no doyoobi-tte tooka-desu-ne.
来週の　土曜日って　十日ですね。
(Next week Saturday is the tenth, isn't it?)

but you can't use *-ttara* in this situation.

Sore-dake
それだけ
(That much)

Yesterday evening Mr. Lerner's landlady, Mrs. Watanabe, came to his home and asked him to give a short speech at a PTA meeting in the neighborhood. Mr. Lerner answered that he wanted to think about it for a couple of days, and today he asked Miss Yoshida for her advice about it. He was not sure if he could speak in good Japanese at a PTA meeting. Then Miss Yoshida said

Sore-dake hanasereba juubun-desu-yo.
それだけ　話せれば　じゅうぶんですよ。

Mr. Lerner thought that the first part, *Sore-dake,* meant "only that," and was wondering why it should be *juubun* (sufficient), when Mr. Takada said *Daijoobu-desu-yo* (It will be okay) so emphatically that he decided to say yes to Mrs. Watanabe.

*　　　*　　　*

The word *dake* is used together with other words and adds the meaning of "the extent" or "the degree"; it does not necessarily mean "only." Whether the extent is great or small depends on the context. For instance, when it is used with a figure, it emphasizes a limit as in

Ato hyaku-en-dake tarinai.
(We need just a hundred yen more.)
Jippun-dake machimasu.
(I'll wait just 10 minutes, no more.)

When *dake* is used with such words as *kore,* *sore* or *are,* it largely depends on the speaker's attitude and context whether the meaning is positive or negative. The expression *sore-dake* can be used both ways as in

> *Sore-dake-ja tarimasen-yo.*
> それだけじゃ　たりませんよ。
> (That much will not be sufficient.)
> *Sore-dake areba juubun-desu.*
> (If there is that much, it will be sufficient.)

In Miss Yoshida's sentence above, *Sore-dake hanasereba* meant "If one can speak as much as you do."

With verbs, *dake* is used to mean "corresponding to" or "enough to" as in

> *Ryokoo-ni iku dake-no okane-wa arimasen.*
> (I don't have the money to go traveling. —*lit.* I don't have money enough to go traveling.)
> *Shidoosha-to iwareru dake-no koto-wa aru.*
> (He is worth being called a leader. — *lit.* He has something that is enough to allow him to be called a leader.)

Onna-dooshi
女同士
(Women together)

Mr. Lerner and Miss Yoshida were invited to the Takadas' last Saturday. After dinner, Mr. Lerner noticed that Miss Yoshida and Mrs. Takada were talking together about something very enthusiastically. When he asked what they were talking about, Miss Yoshida looked embarrassed; it seemed that she did not want to tell him. Then Mrs. Takada smiled and said

Onna-wa onna-dooshi-desu-mono.
女は　女同士ですもの。
(Women can understand each other best.)

while leading her out of the room. Mr. Lerner had heard the expression . . .dooshi several times before, but did not know exactly how it is used.

* * *

According to a recent survey of newspaper kanji, the expression . . .dooshi is one of the most frequently used compounds starting with the kanji doo (同). This expression is popular, but is difficult to put into English. It roughly corresponds to ". . . alone" or "exclusively. . ." For instance, onna-dooshi means "women alone, no men included"; otoko-dooshi can also be used as in

Otoko-dooshi-da-kara kiraku-da.
男同士だから　気らくだ。
(We're all men here, so we can be relaxed.)

76

Thus . . .*dooshi* implies a distinction between those in the group and those outside it — *toshiyori-dooshi* (old people alone) as opposed to young people, and *kodomo-dooshi* (children only) as opposed to parents. When Mrs. Takada said *onna-wa onna-dooshi*, she implied that she did not want men to join the group of Miss Yoshida and herself.

Because of this exclusive nature, the expression . . .*dooshi* is often used to express the unity of people who share something in common. For instance, when most of the company employees have gone traveling together but a few of them have had to stay behind and work, these unlucky ones will say something like

Ikenai mono-dooshi-de ocha-demo nomi-mashoo-ka.
行けない　もの同士で　お茶でも　飲みましょうか。

(Shall we get together and have some tea — those of us who could not go?)

Or, two men who have failed to find dates on a Friday evening may say

Furareta mono-dooshi-de nomi-ni ikoo.
(Let's go drinking together — the two of us who have been refused.)

Ton ton
トン トン
(Knocking)

During the lunch hour yesterday, someone started talking about the sound one makes when walking. He said that he could tell who was going by without looking and just listening to the sound. Mr. Lerner learned various onomatopoeic expressions such as *suta suta* (a quick, light sound), *peta peta* (a slapping sound) and *dosun dosun* (a heavy, thumping sound). Then Miss Yoshida said that she could tell when Mr. Lerner was knocking on the door even when she was inside the room. The secret was very simple; while other people knocked two times as in

Ton, ton, トン トン。

Mr. Lerner knocked three times as

Ton ton ton. トン トン トン。

He had never realized that he knocked differently from the Japanese, and wondered what impression his knocking made on them.

*   *   *

There seems to be no definite pattern among foreigners about how many times they knock on the door at one time, although knocking three times seems to be frequent among Westerners. On the other hand, Japanese usually knock two times; knocking three times or more implies an emergency. When a Japanese is in a room and hears the door knocked on three times or more in succession, he fears that something unusual has

78

happened and hurries to the door. In a sense, foreigners who knock three times can be unintentionally frightening the Japanese around them.

There are several set expressions in Japanese composed of two repeated parts. The opening expression used on the phone is *moshi-moshi* (hello); probably because of this the Japanese often say "Hello, hello" when speaking English, even when they are not particularly anxious or impatient. Another expression is *bai bai*, derived from the English "bye"; in this case too, the Japanese always say *bai bai*.

Makoto-ni tsumaranai mono-desu-ga. . .
まことに つまらない ものですが……
(This is very little, but . . .)

Mr. Lerner and Miss Yoshida were invited to the Takahashis' last Saturday. Both of them brought a gift and handed it to Mrs. Takahashi. Mr. Lerner said politely

Makoto-ni tsumaranai mono-desu-ga . . .
まことに つまらない ものですが……
(This is very little, but please accept it.)

and handed her a box of candy. Since the box was rather small, he used one hand to hand it over, but Mrs. Takahashi took it with two hands and thanked him very politely. And when Miss Yoshida handed over her gift, she held it in two hands although the package of fruit was not large, and Mrs. Takahashi again used two hands to take it. He wondered if he should have used two hands or if only women do so.

After that Mr. Lerner paid careful attention to how the Japanese hand things over, and found that they usually use two hands when they act politely, except when handing over very small things, like name cards.

*　　*　　*

To hand something to someone politely, it is important that even when one hand is used to actually hand it over, the other hand also be used in the action; very often the other hand is placed on it or touches it slightly, as if to confirm the action of handing it over. Namely, when one hand

80

is used to hand over something, the other hand should not be put into a pocket or by one's side.

Politeness has to be supported by consideration to the recipient; the recipient has to be able to take the thing in a proper, easy and pleasant way. For example, when handing over a book or a letter one has to hand it so that the recipient can read it; the recipient should be able to use such things as scissors or pens from the moment they have been handed to him.

The angle is also important; when handing over something with a square shape, one should hand it so that the recipient can take it squarely, not diagonally.

Verbal expressions have to be accompanied by the appropriate non-verbal action. When one uses such polite verbal expressions as *Makoto-ni tsumaranai mono-desu-ga* . . . one also has to use the appropriate polite action; otherwise the recipient will be embarrassed and not know how to respond.

Ojigi
おじぎ
(Bowing)

Mr. Takada introduced one of his acquaintances, a Mr. Yamamoto, to Mr. Lerner the other day. Mr. Lerner gave him his name card and said as usual, *Hajimemashite* (How do you do?). Then Mr. Yamamoto gave him his name card and said while bowing

Hajimete. . . (*lit.* for the first time)

but Mr. Lerner could not hear the rest. He wondered if *Hajimete* can be used in the same way as *Hajimemashite.* Later Mr. Takada explained that Mr. Yamamoto had actually said

Hajimete ome-ni kakarimasu.
はじめて　お目に　かかります。
(How do you do? — *lit.* This is the first time to meet you.)

He realized that *Hajimemashite* is the abbreviation of *Hajimete ome-ni kakarimasu* and also learned that the last half of a sentence can be said in a very low voice that can hardly be heard.

*　　　*　　　*

Polite expressions are often said while bowing. When one says a polite expression with a bow, the last part of the expression is usually said in a low voice because it can be understood without being said clearly. In such expressions as *Hajimete ome-ni kakarimasu, Doozo yoroshiku onegaishimasu* (Glad to meet you or, Please do it for me, depending on the situation — *lit.* Please be good to me) or *Kono tabi-wa makoto-ni ari-gatoo-gozaimashita* (Thank you very much for what you have done for me), the last part is usually said very softly when said while bowing.

When one expresses politeness by bowing in personal situations, one slowly bends one's whole body forward and downward: sometimes one even bends his knees slightly. A quick bow will give an impression of casualness or insincerity, and an abrupt bow will seem childish; to spend the appropriate time bowing, it will help to say, either audibly or inaudibly, such phrases as *ari-gatoo-gozaimashita* or *yoroshiku onegai-shimasu* while bending one's body over.

And one should bow at the same time as the other person does. It is embarrassing to straighten up from bowing long before the other person does. In order to bow in accordance with the other person, it is important to observe him as he starts bowing.

Amari umaku . . . Ikanai-n-desu-ka
あまり　うまく……いかないんですか
(It doesn't go very . . . Well, right?)

Mr. Takada has been working on a project which has to be completed soon. When Miss Yoshida asked him about it yesterday afternoon, he answered

> *Amari umaku . . .*
> あまり　うまく……
> (*lit.* not very successfully. . .)

Then Miss Yoshida said

> *Ikanai-n-desu-ka.*
> いかないんですか。
> (*lit.* It doesn't go, right?)

In a sense Miss Yoshida completed the sentence that Mr. Takada had started and not finished. Mr. Lerner remembered that he had had similar experiences and had felt that the Japanese did so because his Japanese was poor. But now he realized that this custom of finishing up someone's statement is done even between two Japanese and that they do not seem to regard this as impolite.

*　　　*　　　*

In Japanese conversation, finishing up someone's statement is often regarded as a sign of interested participation. Because the Japanese think that a statement can be made up by more than one person, it is natural for one person to leave part of his sentences unsaid and for the other person to finish them.

This is possible only when the rest of the sentence can be guessed, and there are many cases when it can be guessed in Japanese. The use of such adverbs as *amari* (very much) and *doomo* (indeed) usually implies negation or a negative judgment, so it is easy for the listener to complete sentences which include these words. And the use of conjunctions such as *kara* (because), *node* (because) and *kedo* (but) also makes it easy to guess the last part.

The tone with which the statement is said also matters. When the statement is said in one breath and with no sign of encouraging the listener to say anything, the listener usually does not try to finish the sentence. When the first part of a sentence ends with a sustained tone, the listener either finishes it or gives some *aizuchi* (reply words) like *ee* or *hai*.

There remains the question of whether a foreigner should try to finish someone's statement or not. It is basically up to the individual. If he wants to really be accepted as a member of the group he should try to do this and also give *aizuchi* when expected. And it is best to try not to feel offended or unduly patronized when a Japanese listener tries to complete your sentences.

Sonna-ni teeneena kotoba-o tsukawanakute-mo . . .
そんなに　ていねいな　ことばを
使わなくても……
(You don't have to be so polite)

Mr. Lerner was introduced to Mr. Matsu-shita, a company director. He was trying to be as polite as possible, so he said with a bow

Raanaa-to mooshimasu. Hajimete ome-ni kakarimasu. Doozo yoroshiku onegai-itashimasu.
(My name is Lerner. I'm honored to meet you.)

Mr. Matsushita looked a little surprised. He prob-ably had not expected Mr. Lerner to speak such polite Japanese. They talked a while and then when Mr. Lerner was leaving, Mr. Matsushita praised his Japanese and added

Sonna-ni teeneena kotoba-o tsukawanakute-mo ii-n-desu-yo.
そんなに　ていねいな　ことばを　使わなくても
いいんですよ。
(You don't have to use such polite terms.)

Mr. Lerner remembered that he had been told this several times before, and wondered if the Japanese didn't like foreigners to be too polite.

*　　*　　*

Although the number of foreigners who learn Japanese has greatly increased recently, there are still many Japanese who are surprised to hear a foreigner speak polite Japanese. They will often say something like

Sonna-ni teeneena kotoba-o tsukawanakute-mo ii-n-desu-yo.
   or
   Sonna-ni teenee-ni shinakute-mo . . .
   (You don't have to be so polite.)

This is not criticism of the foreigner for being too polite or too formal. They are surprised that a foreigner can speak Japanese so well, and they cannot help admiring a foreigner who can speak it so well.

The Japanese are usually too shy to express their admiration directly. And they are so impressed that they even feel sorry for the foreigner who must have gone through great hardship in order to become able to speak so politely. Thus they end up saying *Sonna-ni. . . .* This expression is, therefore, far from being criticism or a reprimand; in fact, it shows a mixture of embarrassment and admiration.

When your Japanese listener says something like *Sonna-ni teeneena kotoba-o tsukawanakute-mo. . .*, you don't have to worry about being too polite. But it is very important to keep in mind that they will not express themselves when they feel offended or uncomfortable at hearing a foreigner who speaks to them too familiarly or overly aggressively.

Doomo ki-ga tsukimasen-de...
どうも　気が　つきませんで……
(I'm sorry I wasn't attentive enough)

It was rather hot for May but Mr. Lerner and several colleagues were working busily. Mr. Mori, the director of the company, came in and said while sitting down

> *Kyoo-wa iya-ni atsui-nee.*
> きょうは　いやに　あついねえ。
> (Today's awfully hot, isn't it?)

Then Mr. Takada said

> *Doomo ki-ga tsukimasen-de...*
> どうも　気が　つきませんで……
> (*lit.* Indeed I didn't notice, and...)

and hurried to the window and opened it.

Mr. Lerner wondered why Mr. Mori hadn't directly asked someone to open the window. He knew that the Japanese like to express their wishes or requests indirectly toward their superiors, but this time the director of the company had made an indirect request of his men.

*　　　*　　　*

Some people habitually express their requests indirectly; others sometimes do so. Indirect requests can be understood best between good friends or family members. Two people who share the same experiences can understand each other's wishes without clearly indicating them; the other person can understand what is wanted through an indirect hint or a very short reference to it. And many Japanese seem to find pleasure in being with someone who understands them very well, and will sense their wishes and act to realize them without being asked.

This can also be observed when superiors make requests of their subordinates; some bosses like to do this as Mr. Mori did in the case mentioned above.

When one fails to understand an implicit message, one will often apologize by saying something like

Doomo ki-ga tsukimasen-de.

as Mr. Takada did. This actually means "I'm sorry I wasn't attentive enough." Toward their equals or subordinates, more familiar versions like

Ki-ga tsukanakute gomen(-nasai).

are used.

Odekake-desu-ka
おでかけですか
(Are you going out?)

When Mr. Lerner was passing by Mr. Takahashi's house the other day, he saw Mrs. Takahashi coming out hurriedly. He greeted her saying *Konnichiwa* (Good day) and when she had returned the greeting, he added a phrase he had recently learned

Odekake-desu-ka.
おでかけですか。
(*lit.* Are you going out?)

He learned that this is used to greet one's acquaintances just like *Dochira-e* (*lit.* Where are you going?) and he expected her to say

Ee, chotto.
ええ、ちょっと。
(*lit.* Yes, just a little.)

with a smile. But Mrs. Takahashi did not seem to appreciate his effort, and he wondered if this expression had been inappropriate.

*　　　*　　　*

Odekake-desu-ka literally means "Are you going out?" but it is not a question; the speaker has seen the listener and knows that he is going out. It is said to confirm the listener's going out and to express the speaker's happiness about it. The underlying idea seems to be that it is a good thing for anyone to be healthy and wealthy enough to be able to go out. Thus, this corresponds, in a sense, to the English "Have a good time."

Dochira-e is similar to *Odekake-desu-ka* in that it also is not a real question but an indication of neighborly concern. The difference is that *Dochira-e* sounds like the speaker is more concerned about the listener and it is therefore more familiar than *Odekake-desu-ka*.

Odekake-desu-ka and *Dochira-e* are most appropriate when said to someone who is dressed up and going out on a special, usually happy, occasion, rather than leaving to commute to work. They are not usually said to someone who looks unhappy about going out or who has some unhappy business to attend to. Mrs. Takahashi was probably going out on some unpleasant business when she met Mr. Lerner, so *Odekake-desu-ka* did not fit her mood.

Saying *Odekake-desu-ka* or *Dochira-e* serves to give the listener a chance to speak about some happy event in his life. Many Japanese find it psychologically difficult to start talking about their own happiness without being asked. If someone asks them *Odekake-desu-ka*, they can say *Ee, chotto* and add, by way of explanation, something like

Jitsu-wa musuko-no shuushoku-ga kimarimashita-node. . . (As a matter of fact, our son has found a job, so. . .) implying that they are going out to celebrate this.

Watashi-wa doomo hanashi-ga heta-de . . .
わたしは　どうも　話が　へたで……
(I am a poor speaker, so . . .)

Mr. Lerner was asked to give a speech at the wedding reception for Mr. Takahashi's daughter. He wrote out his speech, and asked Mr. Takada to correct it. Mr. Takada went through it, changing a few expressions, and said that he had better apologize for being a poor speaker before starting the speech. Mr. Lerner was reminded that he had often noticed speakers start a speech with an apology like

Watashi-wa doomo hanashi-ga heta-de . . .
わたしは　どうも　話が　へたで……
(*lit.* I am indeed poor at giving a speech, so . . .)
  or
Saisan okotowari-shita-n-desu-ga . . .
(*lit.* I asked to be excused several times, but . . .)

He had felt that these remarks were not always true because the speeches that followed were very often fine ones. He wondered why the Japanese like to apologize even when it is not necessary.

*　　　*　　　*

Many Japanese speakers start their speech with an apology; most often they apologize for being a poor speaker; sometimes they apologize saying that they have not had sufficient time to prepare; and sometimes they say that there must be more appropriate persons to make the speech but somehow they had ended up being chosen. Mr. Lerner was right in thinking that these remarks are not always true; the speakers can be good speakers and they know that themselves. But these apologies are not given as facts but as a kind of opening remark; they are considered to be a necessary step that one should go through, especially on formal occasions.

These opening remarks are helpful in that the listeners can get ready for the speech and that, moreover, the speaker himself can get ready for his speech. In fact, *Watashi-wa doomo hanashi-ga heta-de . . .* actually performs a function similar to such remarks as "I'm glad to be able to speak to you today."

The length of such opening remarks varies depending on the individual, and it seems that shorter ones are welcomed by younger or busy people.

It would be good for a foreigner giving a talk or speech in Japanese to make some short apologetic remark about his Japanese as in

Nihongo-ga fujuubunna-node okikigurushii tokoro-mo aru-to omoimasu-ga . . .

(*lit.* My Japanese is insufficient, so I'm afraid you may at times be uncomfortable listening to me, but . . .)

Owari
おわり
(The end)

The other day Mr. Lerner attended the wedding reception for Mr. Takahashi's daughter and gave a speech. He was able to do fairly well with his speech. He did not make any mistakes and thought he had succeeded, but then when he ended his speech by saying

Kore-de owari-desu.
(This is the end of my speech.)

he felt that something was wrong. He had forgotten that Mr. Takada had crossed out this line when he checked his draft for him.

When he told Mr. Takada about it the following day, Mr. Takada said he was sorry he had not mentioned that it is forbidden to say the word *owari* at a wedding.

*   *   *

At the end of a speech to celebrate a marriage people usually say something like

Doozo sue nagaku oshiawase-ni . . .
どうぞ　末　ながく　おしあわせに……
(May you be happy together for many years to come.)

Words like *owari* are regarded as taboo for a wedding because they suggest the end of the marriage; other expressions like *ohiraki* (*lit.* opening) are used to close a wedding party.

The avoidance of words meaning 'the end" is, however, seen on ordinary occasions, too. Except for very formal occasions, the end of a meeting is not always announced clearly. People often just say *Ja, kore-de* (*llt*. Well, with this), leaving out the phrase meaning *owarimasu* (we will conclude the meeting) or, they often just bow. Foreigners sometimes complain that it is difficult to know whether a meeting has ended or not; it sometimes seems as if people just gradually start leaving without any verbal notice. And when Japanese have gathered and drunk together and are ready to leave, they often avoid words like *owaru* (to end) or *kaeru* (to go home) and will use the words like *ohiraki*, as if closing a wedding party. It is as if they do not like the idea of "ending" their meeting, just as they hate to think of a marriage ending.

'Makoto'-to 'Kobayashi-san'
「まこと」と「小林」さん
(Makoto vs. Kobayashi-san)

Mr. Makoto Kobayashi is the youngest worker in the office where Mr. Lerner works. Although people call each other by their last names at work, Mr. Kobayashi is called "Makoto" as if he were everybody's younger brother.

The other day Mr. Lerner and several other colleagues were invited to the Kobayashi house. Makoto's parents welcomed them warmly and expressed their thanks to them for being kind to Makoto. After dinner, when having tea together, Mr. Lerner wanted to say something nice about Makoto and started saying

Makoto-wa totemo yoku hataraku-n-desu . . .
「まこと」は……
(Makoto is a very hard worker.)

But the parents did not seem to like this. While Mr. Lerner was wondering if he should go on or not, Miss Yoshida hurriedly added, as if to cover Mr. Lerner's blunder

Kobayashi-san-wa . . .
「小林さん」は……

Mr. Lerner realized then that he had been rude in saying "Makoto" without any term of respect.

* * *

The use of terms of respect varies according to the situation; a term that is appropriate within a group will not always be appropriate in another situation. Mr. Kobayashi is called "Makoto" by

96

his colleagues, but he has to be referred to differently when he is in another group. When referring to him in his parents' presence, his position as their son must be considered. Calling him "Makoto" in the presence of his parents sounds as if Makoto is not valued very highly by his colleagues.

This distinction between "in-group" terms and "out-group" terms is strictly observed. A male high school teacher will usually call his students by their last names without terms of respect as "Yoshida," "Takahashi," etc. But when he talks with their parents he will use *kun* with either the last name or the first name of the male students and *san* with those of the female students.

'Doozo'-to 'Onegai-shimasu'
「どうぞ」と「おねがいします」
(Please vs. I request it)

The other day Mr. Lerner visited Mr. Okada at his office. When he arrived, Mr. Okada was not in his room, and his secretary took him to the room where he was working. She asked Mr. Lerner to follow her, saying

Kochira-e onegai-shimasu.
こちらへ　おねがいします。

He understood that she meant "Please come this way." He had learned that in polite expressions such verbs as "come" and "go" are often left out if they can be understood from the situation. But this expression *Kochira-e onegai-shimasu* was not familiar to him. He wondered if she could have said *Kochira-e doozo* instead.

*　　　*　　　*

When making requests politely, *onegai-shimasu* is often used without explicitly indicating an action. To ask someone to write down his name, for example, one often says

Koko-ni onegai-shimasu.

meaning "Please write it here." Verbs other than "write" can also be left out; *Koko-ni onegai-shimasu* can mean *Koko-ni oite-kudasai* (Please put it here) or *Koko-ni tsukete-kudasai* (Please attach it here), too.

Doozo is also used without a verb as in *Kochira-e doozo* (Please come this way) or *Kochira-ni doozo* (Please write it here) or (Please put

98

it here). The difference between the two is that while *onegai-shimasu* implies a request (it is derived from *negau*, to ask or to implore), *doozo* implies a recommendation as to the means of achieving the listener's wishes.. Therefore *doozo* is appropriate in such cases as showing a visitor to the reception room or asking someone to sit down. On the other hand, *onegai-shimasu* is used to ask someone to do a favor. Mr. Okada's secretary used *onegai-shimasu* because she felt that she was asking a favor of Mr. Lerner in taking him to another room. Another person might have used *doozo* in the same situation.

Soo ossharazu-ni . . .
そう　おっしゃらずに……
(Please don't say that)

Mr. Okada took Mr. Lerner to a bar after business discussions the other evening. Mr. Okada kept filling Mr. Lerner's small *sake* cup. When Mr. Lerner said he did not want any more, Mr. Okada said, while continuing to try to pour *sake* into his cup

> *Maa, soo ossharazu-ni . . .*
> まあ、そう　おっしゃらずに……
> (*lit.* Well, don't talk that way, but . . .)

Mr. Lerner remembered that he had often heard Mr. Takada and other colleagues say

> *Maa, soo iwanaide . . .*
> まあ、そう　言わないで……
> (*lit.* Well, don't say so, but . . .)

while offering drinks. He wondered if these two expressions actually mean "Drink more."

* * *

Soo iwanaide and *Soo iwazu-ni* literally mean "Without saying so" or "Don't say so." . . .*naide* and . . . *zu-ni* both mean "don't . . . and"; the difference is that . . . *zu-ni* sounds a little more formal than . . . *naide*. And *ossharanaide* or *ossharazu-ni* are more polite than *iwanaide* or *iwazu-ni*.

After these expressions, phrases meaning "accept my offer" are implied. Sometimes this phrase is included as in

Soo iwanaide moo ippai.

(*lit.* Have another cup without saying that; *nonde-kudasai* — please drink — is usually left out.)

These phrases are used to urge someone to accept the speaker's offer. This offer is not limited to food or drinks; it can be pay or other form of remuneration. Besides this use when giving a gift, they are also used when urging someone to agree to do work considered honorable or difficult. When someone says that a job is too big or too difficult for him, these phrases are used to urge him to overcome his reserve.

Thus the more appropriate English equivalent would be, "Don't be so reserved." This kind of expression is useful when one has to urge someone to accept any kind of offer. The Japanese often refuse an offer at first even when they actually want to accept it, as it is regarded as childish to sound too ready to accept an offer, especially when the offer is an honor or likely to inconvenience the offerer.

Moshi-moshi
もしもし
(Hello)

Mr. Lerner has come to be able to handle daily conversation in Japanese easily, but still has some difficulty talking on the phone in Japanese. The other day he had an embarrassing experience when he was talking with Mr. Okada on the phone.

He was discussing business with Mr. Okada and had to think about something, so he remained silent for a short time. Then Mr. Okada said.

> *Moshi-moshi.* もしもし。
> (Hello.)

as at the beginning of a call. So he said *Moshi-moshi* too, and waited for Mr. Okada to say something. But this time he didn't answer immediately. So Mr. Lerner said *Nan-desu-ka* (What is it?), and Mr. Okada sounded as if he were embarrassed.

*　　　*　　　*

Moshi-moshi is usually learned as an expression used to start a telephone conversation, but it is actually a phrase to get someone's attention, so it can be used in the middle of a telephone conversation or at any time one finds it necessary to get someone's attention. For instance, when someone has dropped something on the street, one can say

> *Moshi-moshi, nanika ochimashita-yo.*
> もしもし、なにか　落ちましたよ。
> (Excuse me, you dropped something.)

102

When Mr. Lerner was thinking silently while talking on the phone, Mr. Okada must have worried if something had happened, and said *Moshi-moshi* to get Mr. Lerner's attention. It was appropriate for Mr. Lerner to have answered *Hai*. The answer to *Moshi-moshi* is *Hai*, not *Moshi-moshi*. Answering *Moshi-moshi* with *Moshi-moshi* in this case is embarrassing.

Another thing about telephoning in Japanese that puzzles foreigners is that there is no set expression to indicate the end of a telephone conversation. When telephoning in English, one says "Good-bye" to indicate that he is finished talking, but *Sayonara* is not always used in Japanese telephone calls. One often says *Ja*, or *Ja, mata*, and sometimes the foreigner finds it difficult to tell if the conversation has ended or not. When talking politely, *Shitsuree-shimasu* is used. In this way, similar expressions are used to end a telephone conversation and to part from someone in person.

Wakatte-imasu
わかっています
(I know!)

Mr. Lerner's colleagues are usually polite and seldom show any anger, but yesterday he had a chance to observe one of those rare occasions when they showed displeasure. Mr. Kato, the section chief, often repeats his directions or instructions. When he started repeating his instructions as usual to Miss Yoshida, she seemed irritated and said

Wakatte-imasu.
わかっています。
(*lit.* I am in the state of understanding it.)

Then Mr. Kato looked very displeased and stared at her with an angry look. Mr. Lerner wanted to ask her about it later, but she looked as if she didn't want to talk about it.

*   *   *

The expression *Wakatte-imasu* means that the speaker knows something already, and it often implies that he does not want to hear any further explanation of it. Therefore it is impolite and squelching to say *Wakatte-imasu* to someone who is explaining something to you with kind intentions. When one wants to indicate that one has understood what was said, one should say

Wakarimashita.
わかりました。
(I understand, *lit.* I understood)

instead.

Needless to say, the tone with which these expressions are said also makes a difference. *Wakarimashita* can be impolite if it is said in an irritated tone, and *Wakatte-imasu* can be appropriate when one wants to assure someone that one understands his problem very well. But basically, *Wakarimashita* is the most appropriate answer to someone's well-meant explanation.

Sometimes foreigners say *Wakarimasu* meaning "I understand," but this is not appropriate when one wants to indicate that one has understood someone's explanation. *Wakarimasu* means "Your situation can be understood" or "I can understand how you feel." It is usually said as an expression of sympathy. It is a typical expression used to comfort someone who is complaining about others.

Tsukaimasu-ka
使いますか
(Are you going to use it?)

   Mr. Lerner invited Mr. Takada, Miss Yoshida and several other colleagues to his house the other day. Since it was a hot day, he prepared some *oshibori* (wet towels) for them, and handed one to Mr. Takada saying

   Oshibori, tsukaimasu-ka.
   おしぼり、使いますか。

meaning "Would you like to use a wet towel?" Mr. Takada thanked him and took it. But when he handed one to Miss Yoshida saying the same phrase, she said that *Tsukaimasu-ka* somehow sounded strange. The others agreed and said

   Tsukaimasen-ka.
   使いませんか。
   (Won't you use it?)

is more appropriate. Mr. Lerner realized then that when he had used . . . *masu-ka* in inviting someone to do something, he should have used . . . *masen-ka* instead.
   In the case above, *Tsukaimasu-ka* can be easily understood from the situation, but *Tsukaimasen-ka* is more appropriate to invite someone to use something. Generally speaking, when offering something, . . . *masen-ka* is more appropriate; for instance, when one invites someone to go out together, one says

   Issho-ni irasshaimasen-ka.
   いっしょに　いらっしゃいませんか。

or
Issho-ni ikimasen-ka.
(Won't you go with me?)

Saying *Issho-ni irasshaimasu-ka* or *Issho-ni iki-masu-ka* sounds as if the speaker just wants to know if someone is going out or not, rather than inviting him.

In the same way, when offering food or drink, it is more appropriate to say *Nomimasen-ka* (Won't you drink some?), *Tabemasen-ka* (Won't you have some?) or politely, *Meshiagari-masen-ka* (Would you like to have some?). Asking someone to have a cup of tea saying *Ocha nomimasu-ka* sounds as if one is rather unenthu-siastic about offering the tea.

Hima-ga aru-n-desu-ka
ひまが　あるんですか
(Is it that you have free time?)

Mr. Lerner wanted to ask Miss Yoshida to type a letter for him, but he was rather late in completing his draft, so he wondered if she might not find it inconvenient. So he first asked her

Hima-ga aru-n-desu-ka.

meaning "Do you have some time free?" Instead of replying right away Miss Yoshida asked him why he had asked her that. When he explained what he would like to ask of her, she said she could do it, but he felt that somehow his expression had been inappropriate.

*　　　*　　　*

To find out if Miss Yoshida was free or not, Mr. Lerner should have said

Hima-ga arimasu-ka.
ひまが　ありますか。

instead of *Hima-ga aru-n-desu-ka.* Asking *Hima-ga aru-n-desu-ka* implied that Mr. Lerner had seen her looking idle or killing time or something of the sort, so naturally Miss Yoshida felt a little offended by it.

The form . . .*n-desu-ka* presupposes some situation that causes the speaker to raise the question. While *Hima-ga arimasu-ka* corresponds to "Do you have some free time?" *Hima-ga aru-n-desu-ka* can be paraphrased as "I see you are idle; is it because you have free time now?"

In the same way, *Dareka kuru-n-desu-ka* (Is it

that you are expecting a visitor?) will be said to tease someone who is cleaning his room unusually carefully or looking frequently at his watch.

Since . . .*n-desu-ka* presupposes a certain situation, it cannot be used when one is simply asking for information. For instance, when you meet someone on the street and ask how he is, you should say *Ogenki-desu-ka* (Are you fine?) If you say

Ogenkina-n-desu-ka,

the listener will feel embarrassed and wonder what situation you are referring to. *Ogenkina-n-desu-ka* implies something like "I heard you were sick; I'm surprised that you look so well" or "I notice you are working hard; are you recovered now?"

Moo ichido itte-kudasai
もう いちど 言ってください
(Please say it again)

The other day Mr. Lerner and Miss Yoshida were invited to Professor Takahashi's house. When they were talking after dinner, Mr. Lerner could not understand something Professor Takahashi had said, so he said

> *Moo ichido itte-kudasai.*
> もう いちど 言ってください。
> (Please say it once more.)

Professor Takahashi looked slightly embarrassed for a moment, then kindly repeated what he had said. Mr. Lerner suspected that his expression had been somehow inappropriate, but he didn't know what he should have said instead.

*   *   *

Moo ichido itte-kudasai is a grammatically correct sentence, and it is appropriate for a teacher or student to use in the classroom. But in social situations, various other means are used instead when one wants to have someone repeat what he has said.

First of all, nonverbal expressions are particularly important in this case. In polite conversation, one first indicates that he has not understood with his facial expressions or by the absence of *aizuchi* (confirming words). Very often the speaker will sense from these signs that the listener has not understood and repeat what he has said before he is verbally asked to do so. Or, one says *Anoo. . .* in a hesitant way. Sometimes one says *Ha?* with a slightly rising tone. *Sumima-*

sen-ga. . . is all right, but is not used as often as *Anoo.* . . or *Ha?* And while saying these expressions, one usually leans forward as if to listen more carefully. If one says *Ha?* while leaning back, it will seem strange; and if *Ha?* is said with a sharply rising tone, one will sound as if he is criticizing the speaker.

Needless to say, in informal speech or conversation between good friends, one can say *Moo ichido itte* (Say it again) or *Moo ichido* (once more). Or, one sometimes says *E?* or *Naani?* (What?) or *Nan-da-tte* (What was that?) to have the speaker repeat his statement. But in polite conversation, one avoids directly asking the listener to repeat something. One sometimes tries to confirm his understanding by asking indirect questions, and when he has to have the speaker repeat his statement, he uses various expressions both verbal and nonverbal, as mentioned above. In polite conversation, saying *Moo ichido itte-kudasai* will sound strange, and it can sound as if one is implying "Do you know what you are saying?" or "Do you really mean what you have said?"

Dakara. . .
だから……
(So,. . .)

Mr. Lerner visited Mr. Takada last Saturday. When he was leaving, Mr. Takada said he would go to the station with him for a walk. Then Mrs. Takada asked her husband to buy a tube of toothpaste at a supermarket near the station. When they were about to leave the house, Mr. Takada asked his wife what size he should buy. Then she said

Dakara itsumo-no chiisai-no-desu-yo.

(*lit.* Therefore, it's the smaller one we always use.)

Mr. Lerner was interested in this use of the word *dakara*. In this case it does not mean "because of that" or "therefore." He remembered that people sometimes use it when they repeat an explanation and wondered if this was merely a sign of repetition.

* * *

Dakara by itself means "because of that," "so" or "therefore," and is used as in:

Ame-ga furisoo-desu-yo. Dakara kasa-o motte-ittara doo-desu-ka.
(It look like it's going to rain, so why don't you take your umbrella with you?)

But sometimes *dakara* is used when there seems to be no preceding indication of the reason. In Mrs. Takada's case above, her husband had simply asked what size he should buy, so phrases meaning "so" or "therefore" do not seem to be appropriate. Actually she was referring, not to her husband's question, but to some situation that was not verbally mentioned. The situation could be that he had already asked the same question or that they had already talked about it. In this case *dakara* can be paraphrased as "you don't listen to me carefully, so I have to repeat my instruction" or "you always say smaller ones are better *so* I'm asking you to buy a smaller one."

Dakara is often used in this way. When the speaker feels irritated about having to repeat an explanation, he often starts his explanation with this word as in:

Dakara sore-wa sakki-mo itta toori. . .
だから それは さっきも 言った とおり……
(So, that's just as I told you a while ago. . .)

And its politer version *desukara* is also used in the same way. A salesman may try to overcome a potential purchaser's doubt about some merchandise by saying

Desukara sono ten-wa mattaku goshinpai gozaimasen.
(So, there's no need to worry about that at all.)

Kaite-kudasaimashita
書いてくださいました
(He kindly wrote it for me)

Professor Takahashi is a good calligrapher, so Mr. Lerner asked him to write something for him. The professor first declined, saying that he was not that good, but finally wrote the Chinese character meaning "perseverance" for him with a big brush. Mr. Lerner liked it very much and hung it on the wall behind his desk at the office. Miss Yoshida immediately noticed it and asked about it, so he explained saying

Takahashi-sensee-ga kaite-kudasaimashita.
高橋先生が　書いてくださいました。
(Professor Takahashi kindly wrote it for me.)

But at the same time he wondered if he should have said

Takahashi-sensee-ni kaite-itadakimashita.
高橋先生に　書いていただきました。
(*lit*. I received from Professor Takahashi the favor of writing it.)

He had learned that both expressions meant the same thing, but wondered if there wasn't some difference between them.

*　　　*　　　*

The two expressions . . . *ga kudasaimashita* and . . . *ni itadakimashita* are used to describe the same action: someone giving something, usually to the speaker. When someone has done some action for the speaker, he can say either

114

. . . *ga* . . . *te-kudasaimashita* or . . . *ni* . . . *te-itadakimashita*. The less polite expressions *kuremashita* and *moraimashita* are also used in the same way.

Both . . . *ga kaite-kudasaimashita* and . . . *ni kaite-itadakimashita* are used to express the speaker's gratitude toward the person who has written something for him. Mr. Lerner could have said . . . *ni kaite-itadakimashita* as well as . . . *ga kaite-kudasaimashita*. The speaker's attitude is, however, different in the two expressions. When saying . . . *ga kaite-kudasaimashita*, the speaker emphasizes the writer's being kind, whereas when he says . . . *ni kaite-itadakimashita* he is more concerned with himself having received a favor. Thus if one were to distinguish between the two expressions, *Sensee-ga kaite-kudasaimashita* corresponds to "He kindly wrote it for me," whereas *Sensee-ni kaite-itadakimashita* corresponds to "I received from him the favor of writing it." The expression used depends on the situation or how the speaker wants to describe the fact.

Sen-en-mo daseba . . .
千円も　出せば……
(If you pay 1,000 yen . . .)

Mr. Lerner noticed that Mr. Takada had a new lighter. Since it was a very smart one, he complimented him on it. Miss Yoshida also noticed it, admired it, and asked if it was very expensive. Mr. Takada replied no, and added

Sen-en-mo daseba doko-demo kaemasu-yo.
千円も　出せば　どこでも　買えますよ。
(You can buy it anywhere if you pay 1,000 yen.)

Then Miss Yoshida said

Sen-en-mo suru-n-desu-ka.
千円も　するんですか。
(Does it cost as much as 1,000 yen?)

Mr. Takada smiled and said that she knew very little about the cost of lighters. And Mr. Lerner wondered whether the two *mo*s used by Mr. Takada and Miss Yoshida were the same or different.

*　　　*　　　*

The particle *mo* added to words indicating amounts implies the speaker's evaluation of the amount. For instance, *sen-en-mo* can mean either "only 1,000 yen" or "as much as 1,000 yen." Mr. Takada used it, in the conversation above, to mean "only 1,000 yen," because he felt that 1,000 yen was a small amount to pay for a lighter. On the other hand, Miss Yoshida said *sen-en-mo* to imply that 1,000 yen seemed to her a large

116

amount of money for a lighter.

Whether *mo* is used positively or negatively is decided by the context. Very often, when followed by . . . *eba* (if . . .). *mo* means "only." Suppose several people are waiting for someone who is late and wondering if they should stop waiting. Someone may suggest waiting a little longer, saying

Ato go-fun-mo mateba kuru-deshoo.
(He should show up in five minutes.)

In this case the speaker implies that five minutes is rather short. But *mo* means "as much as" when someone says angrily

Go-fun-mo matta-noni kimasen-deshita.
(Although I waited for five minutes, he never showed up.)

About learning Japanese, a teacher may say to a student

Ni-nen-mo yareba joozu-ni narimasu.
(You will become good at it if you study for just two years.)

and the student may say

Ni-nen-mo yaru-n-desu-ka.
(Do I have to study it for two whole years!?)

Kore-mo kekkoo-desu-ga . . .
これも　けっこうですが……
(**This is all right, too, but** . . .)

The other day Miss Yoshida offered to help Mr. Lerner buy a present for his mother. They entered a kimono shop and asked to see their *yukatas.* Miss Yoshida looked at several of them but did not decide on any of them. Mr. Lerner knew that they were too expensive and was about to ask the shopkeeper if they didn't have anything less expensive, when Miss Yoshida said

> *Kore-mo kekkoo-desu-kedo* . . .
> これも　けっこうですけど……
> (*lit.* These are all right, too, but . . .)

in a hesitant tone. Then the shopkeeper brought out several others, including less expensive ones.

* * *

It depends on the individual and the type of store or merchandise whether or not the customer will directly ask for something less expensive saying *Motto yasui-no-wa arimasen-ka* (Don't you have any cheaper ones?). When the customer does not want to mention the price, he can say

> *Kore-mo kekkoo-desu-ga* or
> *Kore-mo kekkoo-desu-kedo* . . .

This expression is used to imply that the speaker is not satisfied with the thing he has been given or shown, without mentioning any reason or defect of the thing itself. For instance, when someone has told you his plan and you do not approve of it, you can show your disapproval by saying

> *Sore-mo kekkoo-desu-ga* . . . or
> *Sore-mo ii-n-desu-ga* . . .
> (That is all right, but . . .)

In social situations where it is not appropriate to denounce something flatly, one uses this expression and waits for the listener to change his proposal. Disapproval is indicated indirectly by the use of *mo* (as well as) and *kedo* or *ga* (but). And the hesitant tone is also important because the purpose of this expression is to invite the listener to offer something else of his own accord.

Yoroshiku
よろしく
(Please be good to me)

Mr. Lerner received a telephone call from Mr. Nakamura, an acquaintance of his, the other day. Mr. Nakamura said that he was coming to the city on business in a few days, and might call on Mr. Lerner at his office. When Mr. Lerner asked for details of his visit, he said he would call again and added

Yoroshiku.
よろしく。

before hanging up. Mr. Lerner thought that *Yoroshiku* must be the abbreviation of *Yoroshiku onegai-shimasu* (Please be kind enough to take care of it), and wondered what Mr. Nakamura wanted him to do for him. When he asked Miss Yoshida about it, she said that it was just like "Good-bye" and he didn't have to do anything."

* * *

Yoroshiku or *Yoroshiku onegai-shimasu* is used to ask the listener to do a favor. When it is used when meeting someone for the first time as in *Hajimemashite. Doozo yoroshiku (onegai-shimasu)* the speaker is expressing his desire to build good relations.

Sometimes the favor is verbally specified as in

Musume-o yoroshiku onegai-shimasu.
(*lit.* Please take care of my daughter.)

which is often said by parents to their daughter's

120

bridegroom and his family. Or, in TV commercials, one sometimes hears another product
of the company referred to as in

   X-*mo yoroshiku.*

meaning "Please pay attention to X, too," or actually "Please buy X, too." The favor is implied
when a salesman says to you after having shown
you his catalogs, *Yoroshiku (onegai-shimasu).*
   Very often *Yoroshiku* is used without specifying the favor, as in the case of Mr. Nakamura's
telephone call. Since Mr. Nakamura is not a
close friend of Mr. Lerner's, Miss Yoshida was
right when she said that he didn't have to do anything in particular for him. But if this was said
between close friends or relatives, the speaker
would expect something to be done when saying
Yoroshiku. That something might be coming to
the station or airport to meet him or having him
stay with them for several days. Thus, the favor
must be determined from the situation.

Nee
ねえ
(Isn't it?)

The other day when Mr. Lerner was eating at a little restaurant near the office, a customer came in, and said to the cook

Hara-ga mata utta-nee.
(Hara hit a home run again, didn't he?)

obviously referring to a popular professional baseball player. Then the cook said

Nee. ねえ。

while continuing his cooking. Mr. Lerner wondered if these two *nee*s are the same or different from the short *ne*, often used in conversation.

*   *   *

While the short *ne* is usually used either to solicit the agreement of the listener or to make sure he has understood what has been said, the long *nee* is used to express the speaker's feelings. The feelings expressed can be of many different sorts, but they are usually ones expected to be shared by the listener. You will most often hear *nee* used at the end of a sentence as in

Sukkari aki-ni narimashita-nee.
すっかり　秋に　なりましたねえ。
(Autumn has now completely come, don't you think?)

Sometimes in conversation the subject of the sentence comes last, as in

122

Komatta mon-desu-nee, sono-hito-wa.
こまった　もんですねえ、あの人。
(He is really annoying, isn't he?)

Nee is also used after phrases as in

Hyakuman-en-mo-nee.
百万円もねえ。
(As much as a million yen!)

Secondly, *nee* is sometimes used alone as in the answer of the cook in the case above. When used alone in this way, it indicates the speaker's agreement or sympathy with the listener. The cook here expressed his agreement with the customer's admiration or surprise about the base-ball player's fine play. You might take it as an abbreviation of

> *Honto-ni soo-desu-nee.*
> (It is indeed so, isn't it?)
  or
> *Mattaku-desu-nee.*
> (Indeed.)

Nee is also used alone to attract someone's attention as in

> *Nee, okaasan.*
> (Hey, Mom.)
> *Nee. Kiite-iru-no.*
> (Say. Are you listening to me?)

The long *nee* is pronounced with a falling tone, and it expresses various degrees of emotion depending on the way it is said. The above two sentences can be irritated or imploring, depending on the pronunciation of *nee*.

Ippiki okorashita
いつぴき　おこらした
(I angered one of them)

Yesterday afternoon during a tea break at the office someone started talking about cockroaches. It seemed everyone was annoyed to some extent or other by these persistent creatures. Someone asked Mr. Lerner about it, so he answered,

Kinoo ippiki-o koroshita-kedo . . .

meaning "I killed one yesterday, but . . ." and was going on to say that there must be many more, when everybody started laughing. Miss Yoshida, as usual, immediately realized what was wrong, and explained it to him. He should have said

Kinoo ippiki koroshita-kedo . . .
きのう　いつぴき　ころしたけど……

but what he actually said sounded like . . . *ippiki okorashita*, which means "I angered one of them." It was funny because it sounded as if he were treating cockroaches like human beings and negotiating with them.

*　　*　　*

Mr. Lerner made two mistakes when he said *ippiki-o koroshita*. One was that the "o" sound in *koroshita* was not pronounced right. He opened his mouth too much when pronouncing it, so it sounded like "a." Those English speakers who pronounce the "o" of "hot" like the "a" of "father" have to be careful when pronouncing the

124

Japanese "o" sound. Otherwise their *kowai* (fearful) will be confused with *kawaii* (cute) and *okoshita* (I aroused it) will sound like *okashita* (I violated it).

The other mistake was the use of the phrase *ippiki-o*. He could have said

> *Sono uchi-no ippiki-o koroshita.*
> (I killed one of those.)

but this sounds rather bookish. It is more conversational to say

> *Ippiki koroshita.*

leaving "*o*" out. Phrases indicating numbers are usually used like adverbs without "*o*" or "*ga*" as in

> *Ocha(-o) ippai kudasai.*
> お茶を　いっぱい　ください。
> (Please give me a cup of tea.)
> *Asoko-ni onna-no-hito(-ga) hitori imasu.*
> (There is a woman over there.)

Homerarechatta
ほめられちゃった
(I was praised)

Last Saturday afternoon Mr. Lerner visited the Takadas. He was having tea with them when their son came home from school and started telling his parents what had happened at school that day. First he said

> *Sensee-ni homerarechatta.*
> 先生に　ほめられちゃった。
> (I was praised by the teacher.)

and explained what he had done. Mr. Lerner was interested in this expression; he wondered why the boy had used it instead of *Sensee-ni homerareta* or *Sensee-ga homete-kureta.*

*   *   *

To express the fact that the teacher had praised him, the boy could have said

> *Sensee-ga homete-kureta.*
> 先生が　ほめてくれた。

This implies that the boy is grateful to the teacher for praising him. *Sensee-ga hometa* is not appropriate because it sounds as if the teacher praised someone else, not the speaker.

The form the boy actually chose was the passive form *homerareta*. The passive form in Japanese usually expresses the speaker being affected by some action, and the speaker's feelings about that are usually negative. Examples of this use are *ame-ni furareta* (I was caught in the rain), *ashi-o fumareta* (someone stepped on my foot),

126

and the like. Saying *Sensee-ni homerareta* implies that the speaker is not completely happy about the praise; he may have been surprised or shocked or perhaps he doesn't like having to try to live up to the teacher's high expectations from now on.

And the boy added *shimau*, as in *homerarete-shimatta*; *homerarechatta* is its contracted form. Expressions with . . . *te-shimatta* or . . . *chatta* express either the comletion of an action or the speaker's regret. All in all, *Sensee-ni homerarechatta* implies that the speaker is rather embarrassed about having been praised by the teacher. The cause of his embarrassment is unclear, but at any rate the Takada boy must be rather sensitive to have chosen this form.

Naraimasen
ならいません
(I won't study it)

The other day Miss Yoshida asked Mr. Lerner if his name has any special meaning. She was obviously referring to the fact that his last name "Lerner" has the same pronunciation as "learner." Mr. Lerner said that he didn't know and added

Demo chittomo nihongo-o naraimasen.

meaning "I can't learn Japanese at all." Miss Yoshida said that was not true because he is studying it very hard. He realized then that *naraimasen* is not an exact equivalent of "don't learn."

*　　　*　　　*

The Japanese verb *narau* stresses the action of studying or making efforts to acquire knowledge as in

Ikebana-o naratte-imasu.
(I am studying flower arrangement.)
Juudoo-o naraimasen-ka.
(Why don't you study judo?)

It does not imply the acquisition of knowledge by studying. If you say

Nihongo-o chittomo naraimasen,

it will mean that you haven't started learning Japanese, instead of meaning "I don't make any progress in Japanese." And if you say

128

Kesshite nihongo-o naraimasen,

you will sound as if you are determined not to study Japanese for some reason, since *kesshite* indicates the speaker's determination.

To express the fact that you cannot easily learn and become good at something, you should say

> *Nakanaka joozu-ni narimasen.*
> なかなか　じょうずに　なりません。
> (*lit.* I don't easily become good at it.)
> or
> *Nakanaka oboeraremasen.*
> (*lit.* I can't easily memorize it.)

For a more sophisticated expression, you can say

> *Nakanaka mi-ni tsukimasen.*
> or
> *Nakanaka mono-ni narimasen.*

It may help to memorize the sentence

> *Naratte-imasu-ga oboeraremasen.*
> (I'm studying it but I can't learn it.)

Ano-hito-no koto-da-kara . . .
あの人の　ことだから……
(Since it is that person . . .)

Miss Yoshida asked Mr. Lerner if she could borrow a book he had been reading the week before. When he answered that he had lent it to Mr. Kato a few days before so she should be able to have it in a few days, she said that she would probably be able to read it this year, and added

Ano-hito-no koto-da-kara.
あの人の　ことだから。
(Since it is that person.)

When Mr. Lerner asked her to explain, she said that Mr. Kato is always late in returning things. Mr. Lerner was interested in the phrase *ano-hito-no koto-da-kara,* and wondered if it was used like a phrase he often heard, *kono-goro-no koto-da-kara* (Since things are like that these days).

*　　*　　*

Ano-hito-no koto-da-kara is used to refer to someone's characteristics which the speaker expects the listener to know. When Miss Yoshida said *Ano-hito-no koto-da-kara,* she expected Mr. Lerner to know that Mr. Kato was late in returning things, or else she was talking to herself rather than to Mr. Lerner.

This expression is used between people who share the same knowledge. For instance, when referring to someone who is late, one may say

Ano-hito-no koto-da-kara, moo kuru-daroo.
(Since he is such a person, he will show up at any moment.)

Or, conversely, one may say

Ano-hito-no koto-da-kara . . .

implying that the person is always late and it will be a long time before he comes. A negative judgment is often left unsaid.

Kono-goro-no koto-da-kara is often used to refer to prices. If someone wonders how much he will need to treat his acquaintance to *sushi*, you might say

Kono-goro-no koto-da-kara, ichiman-en-wa iru-deshoo.

(With the prices nowadays, you will need at least ¥10,000.)

This phrase can refer to things other than prices. If one of your Japanese acquaintances wonders if your friend can also speak Japanese, you might say

Kono-goro-no koto-desu-kara, daredemo su-koshi-wa dekiru-deshoo.

(Since this is such an age, anyone should be able to speak it a little.)

Kyoo-wa taihen yoi otenki-desu-ga
きょうは　たいへん　よい　お天気ですが
(Today is a very fine day, but . . .)

Mr. Lerner went to a lecture by a famous economist last Saturday. When the master of ceremonies first introduced the lecturer, he said

Kyoo-wa taihen yoi otenki-desu-ga, minasama yoku oide-kudasaimashita.
きょうは　たいへん　よい　お天気ですが、
みなさま　よく　おいでくださいました。
(*lit.* Today is a very fine day, but it was very nice of all of you to come.)

Mr. Lerner wondered why he had said . . .*ga* (but). Is the weather being fine contradictory to the audience having come? Or, is the conjunction *ga* used without any particular meaning?

*　　　*　　　*

The use of *ga* or *kedo* can puzzle foreigners. These words are sometimes used to connect two contradictory statements as in

Kyoo-wa dame-desu-ga, ashita-nara dekimasu.
(I can't do it today, but I'll be able to do it tomorrow.)

Zuibun doryoku-shita-kedo, umaku ikanakatta.
(I did my best, but it didn't go well.)

Very often statements ending with these words are used to invite the listener's indication of his or her wishes, as in

Ocha-ga hairimashita-kedo. . .
(*lit.* Tea is ready, but. . .)

which implies "would you like to have some now?" or:

Yamada-wa watashi-desu-ga. . .
(*lit.* I am Yamada, but. . .)

which implies "what can I do for you?"

In the case of the speech, *ga* was used to indicate that the speaker was going to take up a different subject. The weather being fine had no direct relation with the audience being large in number. He just wanted to say that he was happy and grateful to have so many people come. In other words, the phrase ending with . . .*ga* was said as an introduction to his speech. In formal situations, many Japanese like to make some introductory remarks before starting their speech, and *ga* or *kedo* is used to conclude such remarks. Dropping *ga* or *kedo* and just saying *Kyoo-wa taihen yoi otenki-desu. Minasama yoku.* . . would sound strange. And if someone leaves out the introductory remark and just says *Minasama yoku oide-kudasaimashita,* it will sound abrupt or informal.

Ikkagetsu maa juuman-en kakaru-deshoo
一か月　まあ　十万円　かかるでしょう
(It will take 100,000 yen a month, I should say)

At lunchtime yesterday when Mr. Lerner and his colleagues were chatting, someone wondered how much one would need to send his son or daughter to college in a big city. Then Miss Yoshida said

Ikkagetsu maa juuman-en kakaru-deshoo-ne.
一か月　まあ　十万円　かかるでしょうね。
(For a month, I should say, it will take a hundred thousand yen.)

Someone else said it would cost more and some others said it would cost less, and the discussion went on, but Mr. Lerner was interested in the word *maa* that Miss Yoshida had used. He had often heard the Japanese use this word, but he hadn't really understood what it meant.

*　　*　　*

Maa is used in several ways in daily conversation, and the *maa* that Miss Yoshida used in her statement shows the most common use. (Here we will not discuss the *maa* used by women to express surprise, as in *Maa, suteki* (How wonderful!).) This *maa* shows the speaker's hesitancy about giving his or her judgment. Miss Yoshida did not want to sound too sure about the figure she gave. In the same way, one will say

Ano-hito-nara maa daijoobu-deshoo.
(I should think he will be all right.)

134

or

Maa soo-deshoo-ne.

(I guess that's about it.)
まあ　そうでしょうね。

One prefers to sound hesitant for various reasons; it can be a lack of confidence, reserve or consideration toward the listener. One may say, to avoid flatly saying "no,"

Maa, muri-kamo shiremasen.
まあ、むりかも　しれません。
(Well, it might be impossible.)

Eeto may seem to be used in a similar way, but it is used when the speaker is looking for the right word or when trying to recall something, rather than to show hesitancy about stating one's opinion.

Iku-n-ja nakatta
行くんじゃ　なかった
(I shouldn't have gone there)

At lunchtime yesterday someone said that a new coffee shop around the corner was serving coffee very cheap for a few days, and Mr. Takada said he would stop in there on his way home. When Miss Yoshida asked him about it today, he said

Anna tokoro, iku-n-ja nakatta-yo.
あんな　ところ、行くんじゃ　なかったよ。
(*lit.* To a place like that, it wasn't that I should go.)

Mr. Lerner wondered for a moment whether Mr. Takada had actually gone there or not, but from the conversation that followed, he realized that he had.

*　　　*　　　*

The expression . . .*n-ja nakatta* is used to express one's regret for having done something; *iku-n-ja nakatta* means "I shouldn't have gone."

For example, when the sky begins to clear up in the afternoon, people will often say

Kasa-nanka motte-kuru-n-ja nakatta-na.
(I shouldn't have brought my umbrella.)

Conversely, when it has started raining you can say

Kasa-o motte-kuru-n-datta-na.
(I should have brought my umbrella.)

This expression is always used with the past form as in *nakatta* or *datta*. With the present form as in . . .*n-ja nai* or . . .*n-da*, it is used to admonish others as in

> *Iku-n-ja nai.* or *Iku-n-ja arimasen.*
> (Don't go.)

or

> *Sonna koto-o yuu-n-ja nai.* or . . .*n-ja arimasen.*
> (You shouldn't say such a thing.)

Therefore the following two expressions should be clearly distinguished.

1. *Kekkon-nanka suru-n-ja nakatta.*
   結婚なんか　するんじゃ　なかつた。
   (I shouldn't have gotten married.)
2. *Kekkon-nanka suru-n-ja nai.*
   結婚なんか　するんじゃ　ない。
   (You shouldn't get married.)

Tetsudaimashoo
てつだいましょう
(I'll help you)

Miss Yoshida seemed very busy, and Mr. Lerner wondered if he could do anything to help her, so he said

Tasukemashoo-ka.

meaning "Can I help you?" But Miss Yoshida didn't understand, so he corrected himself and said

Tasuketai-n-desu.

meaning "I want to help you." Miss Yoshida understood then and said

Aa, tetsudatte-kudasaru-n-desu-ka
(Oh, will you help me?)

Mr. Lerner wondered what difference there was between *tasukeru* and *tetsudau,* but she was so busy that he refrained from asking her.

* * *

The word *tasukeru* means "to rescue someone in trouble." Therefore, it is appropriate for a person who is about to be attacked by someone to say *Tasukete-kure!* (Help!) or *Tasukete!* (Help! — used by women). Or the mother of a sick child will plead with the doctor saying

Doozo kodomo-o tasukete-kudasai.
(Please help my child.)

138

On the other hand *tetsudau* means "to assist someone with his work." Thus you can say

Yoshida-san-no shigoto-o tetsudaimashita.

to mean "I helped Miss Yoshida with her work."

When offering one's help, it is most common to say

Tetsudaimashoo.
てつだいましょう。

or more politely

Otetsudai-shimashoo.
おてつだいしましょう。

Or, you can also say

Nanika otetsudai-dekiru koto-wa arimasen-ka.
なにか おてつだいできる ことは ありませんか。

to mean "Is there anything I can do to help you?"

Thus *tetsudau* must be distinguished from *tasukeru* in usage. If you said to someone who is in serious trouble and has decided to kill himself

Tetsudaimashoo.

you would sound as if you were going to help him commit suicide!

Motte-tte-kudasai
持ってってください
(Please take it)

Mr. Lerner and his colleagues went on a picnic last Saturday. Miss Yoshida asked him to help her take some food out of her car, which was parked a little way from where they were going to eat. When she took out a paper bag and handed it to him, she said

Kore, motte-tte-kudasai.
これ、持ってってください。

Mr. Lerner thought that she had said "please hold it" (*motte-ite-kudasai*), and stood holding it. After a while she came out of the car and was surprised to see him. She said that she had asked him to take it without waiting for her. Obviously he had made a mistake in comprehending the phrase *motte-tte*.

*　　　*　　　*

The distinction between . . .*te-tte* (. . .and go) from . . .*te-itte*, the *te* form of *iku*, and . . .*te-te* (. . . and be) from . . .*te-ite*, the *te* form of *iru*, is rather difficult for foreigners and they often confuse these sounds both when hearing and pronouncing them. Therefore it was difficult for Mr. Lerner to distinguish between *motte-tte-kudasai* and *motte-te-kudasai*. In romanized writing, the difference seems to be just a matter of adding the "t" sound, but actually this is a stop which takes as much time as any other syllable. The expression *kitte-kudasai* (please cut it) is thus quite different from *kite-kudasai* (please wear it, or please come); while *kite* is pronounced as two syl-

140

lables, *kitte* is pronounced as three.

In order to improve comprehension, it helps to practice listening to and pronouncing such pairs as

shite (do and) して vs. *shitte* しって (know and)

nete (sleep and) ねて vs. *nette* ねって (knead and)

And the dropping of the "i" sound also makes comprehension more difficult. In rapid speech the "i" sound is frequently dropped when the meaning can be clearly understood as in

kaite-imasu　　*kaite-masu* (I'm writing)
kaite-imasen　　*kaite-masen* (I'm not writing)
kaite-inai　*kaite-nai* (I'm not writing)
matte-iraremasen　*matte-raremasen* (I can't be waiting)
motte-itte-kudasai　*motte-tte-kudasai* (please take it).

Sono-kurai
その くらい
(About that much)

During lunchtime yesterday Miss Yoshida had demonstrated a new type of tongue twister and her colleagues were admiring her, when Mr. Kato came in and joined the group. Mr. Takada asked him if he could say it as well as Miss Yoshida did. Then Mr. Kato answered

Sono-kurai. . .
その くらい……
(*lit.* About that much. . .)

While Mr. Lerner was wondering what was to follow this phrase, everybody clapped their hands and Mr. Kato started saying the tongue twister. Mr. Lerner wondered how such a short phrase could convey the meaning that Mr. Kato felt he was able to say it.

* * *

One usage of *kurai* or *gurai*, when added to another word, is to mean "about" or "approximately"; *sen-en-gurai* means "about 1,000 yen." It is used very commonly as in:

A: *Ikura-gurai kakaru-deshoo-ne.*
   (How much will it cost?)
B: *Soo-desu-nee. Juuman-en-gurai kakaru-deshoo-ne.*
   (Well, it will cost about 100,000 yen.)

Another usage of *kurai* or *gurai* is, as in Mr. Kato's answer above, to show that the speaker has a depreciatory judgment of the subject matter. When Mr. Takada implied that the tongue twister was a very difficult one, Mr. Kato implied that it wasn't, denying Mr. Takada's evaluation. After *sono kurai* here, *dekiru-yo* (I can do it easily) is understood and left out.

Similarly, one may say

Sono-gurai wakatte-ru-yo.
そのぐらい わかってるよ。
(I know that much.)

in defiance of the other speaker who seems to regard it as necessary to explain something or to call attention to something. Or, one may say to a friend who hesitantly wonders if he could borrow 10,000 yen,

Ichiman-en-gurai boku-datte kashite-agerareru-yo.
(I can lend you 10,000 yen.)

implying "although you may not expect me to be able to do so." The speaker may be saying this to boast or to get rid of the friend's reserve.

Kuru hazu-desu
来る　はずです
(I expect him to come)

Mr. Lerner and his colleagues decided to go on a picnic next Saturday, and Miss Yoshida allotted food for each of them to bring, but she seemed to forget Mr. Lerner's assignment, so he went to her and asked

Watashi-wa nani-o motte-kuru hazu-desu-ka.

meaning "What am I expected to bring?" Miss Yoshida told him what to bring, and added that he should not have used the word *hazu* because it sounded strange somehow, but she could not explain why.

*　　　*　　　*

The expression . . .*(suru) hazu* is used to indicate the speaker's expectation about something or someone else, as in

Moo kuru hazu-desu.
もう　来る　はずです。
(It's about time he came.)

which implies that the speaker expects someone to come because he has received a call from him and knows what time he is coming or the like. Or, implying that it is already the cold season, one may say

Moo samuku naru hazu-na-n-desu-ga-nee.
(It should be cold now.)

When *hazu* is used, a sentence with no explicit

subject is usually understood to refer to the third person; *kuru hazu-desu* usually means "he/she/it/they is/are expected to come" or rather, "I expect him/her/it/them to come."

Since *hazu* is used to indicate the speaker's expectations toward others, it is not appropriate to use it when referring to someone else's expectation toward the speaker (oneself) as Mr. Lerner did in the case above. In English, it is possible to say "Am I expected to. . .?," but in Japanese, . . . *hazu-desu-ka* is not used to ask about the listener's expectations toward the speaker. To ask someone what he expects of you, you should use other expressions such as . . . *mashoo-ka* (shall I. . .?) or . . . *koto-ni natte-imasu-ka* (*lit.* has it been arranged that. . .?) as in

> *Watashi-wa nani-o motte-kimashoo-ka.*
> わたしは　何を　持ってきましょうか。
> (What shall I bring?)
> or
> *Watashi-wa nani-o motte-kuru koto-ni natte-imasu-ka.*
> わたしは　何を　持ってくる　ことに　なっていますか。
> (What am I supposed to bring?)

Yukkuri shite-itte-kudasai
ゆっくり　していってください
(Please stay longer)

Mr. Lerner visited Professor Takahashi the other day. When he was about to leave, Mrs. Takahashi came in and said

Motto yukkuri shite-itte-kudasai.
もっと　ゆっくり　していってください。
(*lit.* Please take more time and go.)

This expression was not new to Mr. Lerner, but since he had just learned to hear the distinction between *itte-kudasai* (please go) and *ite-kudasai* (please stay), he was sensitive to the addition of *itte*. Why do the Japanese often add *itte* when talking to visitors? Are they anxious to have them leave?

*　　*　　*

It is true that hosts or hostesses often add *itte* to their sentences to a visitor as in

Ocha-demo nonde-itte-kudasai.
お茶でも　飲んでいってください。
(Please have some tea.)
Moo sukoshi asonde-ittara doo-desu-ka.
(Can't you stay a little longer?)
Haha-ni atte-itte-kuremasen-ka.
(Won't you meet my mother?)

These expressions with *itte* are not used toward one's family members or to those who live together; this is limited to host-visitor relations. Literally, . . .*itte* means ". . . and go," but in such statements, the emphasis is not placed on the

146

leaving. This expression is used when the speaker presupposes that the listener is going away after the action. Therefore, rather than "please . . . and go," it should be taken as "please . . . before leaving." This does not indicate that the host is anxious to get rid of a visitor. A good friend will say to you

Enryo shinai-de, nannichi-demo tomatte-ike-yo.
(Don't be reserved. Stay with us as long as you like — *lit.* Stay for any number of days.)

Foreigners who are planning to stay in Japan for a short time are visitors, so the Japanese may say things like

Iroirona mono-o mite-itte-kudasai.
(Please see lots of things before you leave.)

as an indication of hostly good wishes.

GUIDE FOR AVOIDANCE OF
COMMON MISTAKES (2)

The following is a list of basic grammatical items and example sentences accompanied with explanations; this is designed to help those who are studying Japanese avoid making common mistakes. Although the selection of items is based on error analysis, correct model sentences are given first and then the errors are explained later, in order not to impress the reader with wrong usages. In most of items, one or two additional examples are added for reference.

Since space is limited, the list is not a comprehensive one, but we have tried to include basic and typical items with which students are apt to have trouble.

Going through the list will help confirm your knowledge of basic Japanese grammar, and if you want further information on any of the items, we recommend that you refer to either *Nihongo Notes 1, 2, 3 & 4* (abbreviated as NN-1, NN-2, NN-3, NN-4) or *An Introduction to Modern Japanese* (abbreviated as IMJ).

(Nihongo Notes 3 has another list of common mistakes.)

26. INDICATING ABILITY OR SKILL

a) *Nihongo-ga dekimasu.* (I can speak Japanese.)

It is wrong to say *Nihongo-o dekimasu.* One can also say *Nihongo-o hanasu/kaku/yomu koto-ga dekimasu.* (I can speak/write/read Japanese.)

b) *Piano-ga joozu-desu.* (She is good at the piano.)

It is wrong to say *Piano-de joozu-desu.*

(cf. IMJ, p. 132)

27. INDICATING PLACE OF WORK

Booeki-gaisha-ni tsutomete-imasu. (I work for a trading company.)

It is wrong to say *Booeki-gaisha-de tsutomete-imasu.* One can also say . . .*de hataraite-imasu.*

Additional example:

Dochira-ni otsutome-desu-ka. (Where do you work?)

(cf. IMJ, p. 86)

28. INDICATING STARTING POINT

Eki-o dete, kita-e ikimasu. (I go to the north after coming out of the station.)

It is wrong to say *eki-ni deru*, which means "to come out at the station," as in "If you follow this street, you will come out at the station."

Additional example:

Nanji-ni uchi-o demasu-ka. (What time do you leave home? — *uchi-o* is often left out when it can be understood.)

(cf. IMJ, p. 201)

29. INDICATING SPACE THROUGH WHICH AN ACTION TAKES PLACE

Kono michi-o massugu itte-kudasai. (Please go straight along this road.)

It is wrong to say *Kono michi-de itte-kudasai.* Such verbs as *iku, aruku, tooru, hashi-*

ru, and *tobu* (go, walk, pass through, run, and fly) respectively are preceded by "*o*."
Additional examples:

Kono basu-wa doko-o toorimasu-ka. (Where does this bus go through? — *i. e.* What streets does it take?)

Rooka-o hashiranaide-kudasai. (Please do not run in the halls.)

30. BEING ABSENT

Byooki-de gakkoo-o yasumimashita. (I was absent from school because of illness.)

It is wrong to say *Gakkoo(or Kaisha)-kara yasumimashita.*

31. REFERRING TO THE TOPIC OF CONVERSATION

Sono-hito-wa ima doko-ni imasu-ka. (Where is he now?)

It is wrong to use "*ga*" when referring to someone or something that has already been discussed.

Additional examples:

(1) A: *Okyaku-san-ga kimashita-yo. Otoko-no-hito-desu.* (Someone has come to see you — a man)

B: *Sono-hito-wa ima doko-ni imasu-ka.* (Where is he now? — *Sono-hito-wa* can be left out.) *Sono-hito-ga* should not be used.

(2) A: *Dareka-ga kasa-o wasuremashita.* (Someone has left his umbrella.)

B: (pointing to the umbrella) *A, sore-wa Yamamoto-san-no-desu.* (That's Mr. Yamamoto's.) *Sore-ga* should not be used.

(cf. NN-3, pp. 50-1)

32. HEARING SOMETHING

Taiko-no oto-ga kikoemasu-ne. (We hear a drum beating, don't we?)

It is wrong to say *Taiko-no oto-o kikimasu* in this case. The verb *kiku* is used for intentional listening as in *Yoku kiite-kudasai.* (Please listen carefully.)

Additional example:

> *Urusakute hanashi-ga kikoemasen.* (It's so noisy that I can't hear what he is saying. *Kikimasen* or *Kikemasen* should not be used.
>
> (cf. NN-3, pp. 146-7)

33. SEEING SOMETHING

Fujisan-ga yoku miemashita. (We could see Mt. Fuji very clearly.)

It is wrong to say *Fujisan-o yoku mimashita*, which sounds as if you were intentionally taking a good look at Mt. Fuji; saying *Fujisan-ga miraremashita* sounds awkward.

Additional example:

> *Kumotte-ita-node Fujisan-ga miemasen-deshita.* (It was cloudy, so we couldn't see Mt. Fuji.) *Miraremasen-deshita* can also be used.

34. OPENING A DOOR, WINDOW, ETC.

To-o akete-kudasai. (Please open the door.)

It is wrong to say *To-o aite-kudasai* or *Mado-o akimashita*. When opening something, *akeru* is used instead of *aku*. In the same way, *shimeru* is used instead of *shimaru* when closing something.

Additional examples of transitive and intransitive verbs:

> *dentoo(or denki)-o tsukeru* (to turn on a light) — *denki-ga tsuku* (A light is turned on.)
> *dentoo(or denki)-o kesu* (to turn off a light) —*denki-ga kieru* (A light is turned off.)

35. ONE'S DISEASE BEING CURED

Byooki-ga naorimashita. (I am recovered from my illness.)

It is unusual to say *Byooki-o naoshimashita* in this case. The verb *naosu* is used with a doctor curing someone's disease, or when referring to repairing something.

Additional example:

> *Hayaku kaze-ga naoru-to ii-desu-ne.* (I hope your cold will be cured very soon.)

36. COMPLETED ACTION

Uchi-ni kaetta toki, kimono-ni kikaemasu. (I change into kimono when I get home.)

It is wrong in this case to say *Uchi-ni kaeru toki . . .*; then it would sound as if you were wearing kimono on your way home. The *"ta"* form must be used to show the completion of the action of reaching home.

Additional examples:

Eki-e iku toki Yamada-san-ni aimashita. (I met Mr. Yamada on my way to the station.)

Kondo Yamada-san-ni atta toki, watashite-kudasai. (Please hand it to Mr. Yamada when you meet him.)

(cf. NN-1, pp. 34-5)

37. FORMS FOLLOWED BY *TO OMOIMASU*

a) *Atarashii-to omoimasu.* (I think it's new.)

It is wrong to say *Atarashii-da-to omoimasu.*

b) *Soo omoimasu.* (I think so.)

It is wrong to say *Soo-to omoimasu*, although it is correct to say *Soo-da-to omoimasu.* (I think it is so.)

(cf. IMJ, pp. 96, 152-3)

38. IMMEDIATE FUTURE

Kore-kara dekakemasu. (I'm going to leave now.)

It is wrong to say *Kore-kara dekaketeimasu.*

Additional example:

Sugu kimasu. (He's coming very soon.) In this case, saying *Kite-imasu* means that he is already here.

(cf. NN-1, p. 102)

39. ASKING FOR HELP

Tetsudatte-moraitai-to omoimasu. (I'd like him to help me.)

Tetsudatte-hoshii-to omoimasu. (I'd like him to help me.)

It is wrong to say *tetsudai-ga moraitai* or *tetsudai-ga hoshii.*; *. . .ga hoshii* or *. . .ga mo-*

raitai is used with things rather than actions.
Additional example:

> *Oshiete-itadakitai-to omoimasu.* (I'd like you to teach me.) It is wrong to say *Oshie-ga hoshii* when asking for instruction.

40. INDICATING STATE OF BEING
Omoshiroi koto-ga kaite-arimasu. (Something interesting is written.)

It is wrong to say *Omoshiroi koto-o kakima-shita* in this case. The "*te*" form plus *aru* is used when referring to a state of being caused by an action.

Additional examples:

> *Mado-ga akete-arimasu.* (The window is open.)
> *Denki-ga tsukete-arimasu.* (The light is on.)
> *Ofuro-ga wakashite-arimasu.* (The bath is ready — *lit.* is heated.)

(cf. IMJ, pp. 221-2; NN-3, pp. 140-1)

41. INDICATING INTENTION
Sugu yameru tsumori-desu. (I intend to stop doing it soon.)

It is wrong to say *Sugu yameru hazu-desu*, because *hazu* is used to refer to the speaker's expectations about someone or something else.

(cf. IMJ, p. 199; NN-4, pp. 144-5)

42. DESCRIBING AGE
Uchi-no kodomo-wa mada chiisai-desu. (Our child is still very young.)

It is wrong to say *Uchi-no kodomo-wa mada wakai-desu* when referring to a person in childhood. *Wakai* is used for someone in their adolescence or older.

(cf. NN-1, p. 10)

43. HOT WATER
Oyu-o kudasai. (Please give me some hot water.)

It is wrong to say *atsui mizu*; *mizu* and *atsui*

cannot be used together because *mizu* is thought to be something that is not hot.

44. COLD WATER
Tsumetai mizu-o kudasai. (Please give me some cold water.)

It is wrong to say *samui mizu* because *samui* is used to refer to the weather or the air, not something tangible.

(cf. NN-1, pp. 108-9)

45. TAKING A BATH
Ofuro-ni hairimasu. (I'm going to take a bath.)

It is wrong to say *Ofuro-o torimasu.*

46. USING *MONO* WHEN REFERRING TO SOMETHING ABSTRACT
Heewa-to yuu mono-wa ii mono-desu. (Peace is a very fine thing.)

It is wrong to say *Heewa-to yuu koto-wa ii koto-desu* in this case. *Mono* is used with both abstract and concrete things, but *koto* is used with a verb as in:
Heewa-o mamoru-to yuu koto-wa ii koto-desu. (It is a good thing to maintain peace.)
Additional examples:
Aijoo-wa daijina mono-desu-ga, hontoo-ni hito-o aisuru koto-wa muzukashii koto-desu. (Love is very important, but to really love someone is a very difficult thing.) It is wrong to say *aisuru mono* in this case.

47. INDICATING CHANGE IN A STATE OF BEING
a) *Dandan samuku narimasu.* (It will gradually become colder.)

It is wrong to say *samuku-ni narimasu.*
Additional example:
Mae-yori omoshiroku narimashita. (It became more interesting than before.) *Omoshiroku-ni* should not be used.

155

b) *Heya-ga kiree-ni narimashita.* (The room has become more beautiful or cleaner.)

It is wrong to say *kireeku narimashita.*

Additional example:

Tonari-no heya-ga shizuka-ni narimashita. (The next room has become quiet.)

c) *Dandan hanaseru yoo-ni narimasu.* (You will gradually become able to speak better.)

It is wrong to say *Hanaseru-ni narimasu.*

Additional example:

Yoku wakaru yoo-ni narimashita. (I have come to be able to understand well.) *wakaru-ni* should not be used.

d) *Takaku natte, kaenaku narimashita.* (It has become more expensive, so I can't buy it.)

With the negative, either *kaeru yoo-ni narimasen* or *kaenaku narimashita* can be used depending on the situation; the first one stresses the change while the second one stresses the state of being.

48. *SORE-DE*

Okane-ga tarinaku narimashita. Sore-de Yamada-san-ni karimashita. (I ran short of money, so I borrowed some from Mr. Yamada.)

It is wrong to say *sore-dewa* in this case. *Sore-dewa* is used in the meaning "if that is the case."

Additional example:

A: *Moo rokuji-desu-ga.* . . (It's already six now.)

B: *Soo-desu-ka.* . . . *Sore-dewa sorosoro hajimemashoo-ka.* (Is that right? Then shall we start now?)

49. LEAVING UNSAID WHAT CAN BE UNDERSTOOD FROM THE CONTEXT

a) A: *Ashita Kyooto-e ikimasu-ka.* (Are you going to go to Kyoto tomorrow?)

B: *Ee, ikimasu.* (Yes, I am.)

It is awkward to say *Ee, ashita Kyooto-e ikimasu*, unless you want to emphasize *ashita* or *Kyooto*.

b) A: *Sono hon-wa ikura-deshita-ka.* (How much was that book?)

B: *Sen-en-deshita.* (It was 1,000 yen.)

It is awkward to say *Sono hon-wa sen-en-deshita* or *Sore-wa . . .*, unless you want to attract special attention to the phrase or show contrast with other books.

(cf. IMJ, pp. 15-6; NN-1, pp. 120-1)

50. LEAVING UNSAID WHAT CAN BE UNDERSTOOD FROM THE PHYSICAL SITUATION

a) (when offering tea) *Doozo.* or *Ocha-o doozo.* (Please have some tea.)

It is awkward to say *Doozo ocha-o nonde-kudasai* when you are serving tea. *Nonde-kudasai* or *Ocha-o nonde-kudasai* should be left out as one should leave out what can be understood easily from the situation. In the same way, when offering a seat, for example, *Doozo* or *Doozo okake-kudasai* should be used, instead of *Doozo isu-ni okake-kudasai.* If you want to emphasize this chair, rather than others, it is all right to say *Doozo koko-e* or *Doozo koko-e okake-kudasai.*

(cf. NN-1, pp. 66-7)

INDEX TO WORDS, PHRASES AND SENTENCES

159

T